Why Jesus Died

FACETS

Selected Titles in the Facets Series

The Contemporary Quest for Jesus
N. T. Wright

Jesus and Nonviolence: A Third Way
Walter Wink

Who Is Christ for Us?
Dietrich Bonhoeffer

The Call to Discipleship
Karl Barth

*Religion and Empire:
People, Power, and the Life of the Spirit*
Richard Horsley

Why Jesus Died

Gerard S. Sloyan

Fortress Press
Minneapolis

WHY JESUS DIED
Facets edition 2004 edited by Marshall D. Johnson

Scripture translations are the author's or from the New Revised Standard Version Bible, ©1989 by the Division of Christian Education of the National Council of the Churches of Christ in the USA and used by permission.

This volume is an edited excerpt of *The Crucifixion of Jesus* by Gerard S. Sloyan (Minneapolis: Fortress Press, 1995).

Cover image: Detail of *It Is Finished* by Sandra Bowden. Used by permission of the artist. For more information, see www.sandrabowden.com.

ISBN: 0-8006-3693-7

The paper used in this publication meets the minimum requirements of American National Standard for Information Sciences—Permanence of Paper for Printed Library Materials, ANSI Z329.48-1984.

Manufactured in the U.S.A.
08 07 06 05 04   3 4 5 6 7 8 9 10

Contents

Introduction

Jesus of Nazareth in Galilee died on a cross at the hands of Roman justice, probably in the year 30 of the Common Era. Hundreds of thousands were subjected to this cruel punishment before and after him. Yet one is hard-pressed to provide the name of another victim of crucifixion—apart from his companions in life Peter and Andrew—to whom Christian legend has attributed the same fate. Jesus emerges from those myriads of nameless slaves, brigands, and insurgents as "the Crucified."

Others are remembered for the *way* they died: Socrates, Jewish and Christian and Muslim martyrs both named and nameless, the dead of the Nazi Holocaust and other genocides whose sole crime was their peoplehood. Many of these deaths were preceded by the most shameful indignities and tortures. The death of Jesus was hardly unique in its ignominy. He did not, according to the Gospels, survive long on the cross. No carrion birds soared low over his carcass, his lifeblood seeping out to signal imminent death, as commonly happened to those left to die by this form of execution. Millions of innocent victims of political warfare have been subjected to greater tortures than he, as Amnesty International and similar agencies document from month to month. Why, then, is he remembered as if he, uniquely, had died as an innocent victim and in this fashion?

For two reasons, chiefly. The violent deaths of history's great ones—among whom he must be reckoned—are usually a matter of swift dispatch. Few meet their end in as sordid and demeaning a fashion as this, marked by details their devotees then celebrate. Far more important, however, are the cosmic effects attributed to the death of Jesus, to which its actual circumstances are subordinate.

The circumstances of Jesus' death are not subordinate for everyone. They have been made the subject of what can only be called a Christian piety of pain. In this development—not yet evident in the early church—the lacerations of his flesh by flogging, the nails in his hands and feet and the spear that pierced his side, the helmet of spines that indented his skull, and the mocking and spitting became paramount. From the early Middle Ages onward, God's love for a sinful humanity came to be gauged by the amount of pain Jesus endured on behalf of those who, by their sins, deserved it.

The chief actual sufferers from Jesus' death by crucifixion have been—paradoxically—not Christians but Jesus' fellow Jews. From an early period—the mid-second century can be documented—the apparent complicity in this death of the priestly leadership of the Jerusalem Temple with the Roman prefect of Palestine was extrapolated and extended by Christians to the whole city, the whole land, and before long the whole people. Jews have suffered untold indignities at the hands of Christians, even to their liquidation, as a result of the way Jesus died. So much is this the case that the image of a cross bearing Jesus' body—a crucifix—is taken by Jews as being, far from the sign of the redemption of the human race that it is for Christians, a reproach on them for killing God's Son. For this deed Christians devised the term *deicide,* the murder of deity. Efforts of the latter half of the twentieth century to convince Jews that no such symbolism is intended by the crucifix have been largely unavailing.

The four Gospels present Jesus' crucifixion in close conjunction with his being raised from the dead. This joining of the two is as much theological as chronological. When Christians conceive his death and resurrection correctly it is as one mystery of faith, not two. Paul is the earliest known interpreter of the meaning of his death. In seven letters that are certainly Paul's, spanning the years 50–57 C.E., he never uses the phrase "death and resurrection." It is clear, however, that his use of the terms "death," "cross," "death on the cross," or "word of the cross" always implies resurrection, often in a phrase that occurs nearby. In the same way, his use of "resurrection," "glory," or "splendor of the Father" when referring to Christ is a way of including the death in shame that preceded it.

When the *risen* Christ is displayed iconographically on crosses in the sanctuaries of churches of the Catholic tradition of the West, Jews tend to be puzzled but pleased by the substitution. Some Christians are displeased by what they take to be a de-emphasis of Jesus' redemptive death, while other Christians deplore any imaged representation at all. Such glorified Christs on the cross are, of course, an attempt to say that crucifixion-resurrection is the one mystery of faith.

For anyone who takes Judaism or Islam or Christianity or Hinduism or Buddhism seriously, it is all but impossible to explore dispassionately the central matter that constitutes it. *Passion* connotes undergoing something, being gripped by something. It need not be one's feelings or emotions. Intellectual passion is real and very strong. In scholarly explorations of the crucifixion of Jesus—as considered separately from his resurrection by both religious believers and nonbelievers in it—it is impossible to discover dispassion, either intellectually conceived or as it touches the whole person. Too many claims have been made for this death, and too many lives have been lost both in witness to its meaning and as a tragically misguided conclusion from its meaning, for this dispassion to be possible.

Is the cross the symbol of a necrophilic cult? Does it accept suffering willingly while millions go convinced, religiously or otherwise, that life's main purpose should be to avoid suffering? Many have the conviction that pain should not be piously reflected on but eliminated, whether by meditative transcendence or physical or mental cure. Does faith in the cross relieve the burden of sin or does it create guilt for sins? All such questions prove inescapable for those who study Jesus' *death* and the effects it has had, whether they were reared in a religious tradition or a religious vacuum.

Compounding this is an all but universal interest in the *life* of the man Jesus by anyone who has heard of him. Jews are an exception, because Jesus' followers have caused them so much anguish. They have long ago classified him as a teacher of the late Second Temple period who is of little interest to them. Any persons who have come to know his teaching intimately, although not as believers, can be puzzled at the emphasis put on his death when it seems to them that his life is what matters. How can one see his life, teaching, and example, on the one hand, and his death and resurrection, on the other, as a single fabric? The evangelists did not seem to integrate them successfully, nor did Paul nor the Epistle to the Hebrews nor Revelation. They all left to the later church the problem of relating Jesus' teaching career to the tragic events of his last few days. Outsiders to Christianity perceive the problem. Those within frequently do not.

It is certainly possible to bracket all theological consideration of the death of Jesus and attend to it as an event in human history. This way lies open to the historically sophisticated, whether they believe in Jesus' death as a religious mystery or not. They cannot lay their faith or unfaith, their prejudices, or their passions completely aside. What they can do is follow the canons of modern historiography developed since the Enlightenment, more especially since 1800. It is essential, at the same time, that they be aware of the canons of ancient historiography.

Matthew, Mark, Luke, John, Paul, John of Patmos, and the anonymous others intended to write history in the fashion of biblical historians. The resurrection of Jesus from the dead was witnessed by no one, they say. They report that once he was raised he appeared in an altered, glorified state—and to believers only. The writers make no claim that this new life of his was history in the ordinary sense; rather the opposite.[1] But when it came to his apprehension by the temple authorities or the Roman soldiery in an olive orchard by night, his appearance before religious and civil authority ending in capital sentence, and his being submitted to the tortures attendant on crucifixion, a historical account was undoubtedly intended.

The Gospel narratives were based on a sum of historical reminiscences. Like all ancient history, these had been elaborated with the passage of time. History in the Gospels is not a bald factual chronicle. It encompasses an imputation of motives and states of mind, although only John of the four presents Jesus' thoughts and intentions. In this the Gospels resemble all *ancient* history and much of modern.

In brief, the circumstances of Jesus' death are open to inquiry because a number of ancient documents originating in a community sympathetic to him recorded them. No cross-reference with other writings is possible until mentions in pagan polemical literature and the Talmud begin to occur. There is nothing unusual in this. We do not possess primitive testimony to any religion from outside it, only from within. An old challenge asks why no mention of Jesus' execution exists in imperial records if it were so important. This challenge rests on a number of assumptions, some of them false and the rest doubtful, for example, that *any* correspondence from Pilate to Rome is extant, that he thought the victim important enough to report his death by name, and that as a prefect of the equestrian order he would have been expected to send forward an account of all the insurgent colonials he sent to the stake and crossbeam.

The place to begin this inquiry appears to be the only narrative accounts we have of Jesus' last days, the Gospels. Paul, a quarter of a century after the event, frequently mentions that Jesus died this way, but he provides no particulars. As background to the trial and crucifixion accounts, a summary of what is known of Roman and Jewish justice is in order; more than that, of who was condemned to crucifixion in the ancient world and on what charges. The risen-life narratives need to be reported on but not with the same detail as the trial and crucifixion accounts, since data of the same historical order are not in question. This inquiry into history will be the subject of chapter 1.

A second aspect of this inquiry will be the interpretation put on Jesus' death by those who believed in his resurrection. Luke's volume two, titled much later "The Acts of the Apostles," purports to convey the way Jesus' disciples understood these events a short seven weeks after they occurred. The public proclamation of him as dead and risen, made possible, as Acts maintains, by the action of the Spirit proves to be a set of apologetic arguments that had been crafted over the course of decades. These were framed on the basis of the Greek translation of the Bible (the Septuagint), which only some pilgrims in a Jerusalem crowd would have been at home in. The speeches of Peter in the first part of Acts clearly come from a much later time. A great variety of theological understandings of the meaning of crucifixion-resurrection can be found in the New Testament, not just the Lukan theological history written in the late first century. It is important to try to discover what underlay the decision—evidently taken very early—to find virtue in Jesus' ignominious death. What is the likeliest explanation of the disciples' decision not simply to acknowledge that their champion had been condemned as an enemy of the state but to boast of his shameful end? What led them to claim for it the power, if not to reverse world history, at least to steer it in an entirely new direction; to make reparation for all disordered human behavior and enable the entire race to live a new, Godlike existence? The origins of the death of Jesus as "saving" and the several ways in which this belief has been expressed theologically should come next in order.

The third part of this book will review the variety of understandings Christians of the first five centuries have derived from or placed upon the biblical data. It is put that way and not "the New Testament data" because the Scriptures of the Jews were taken to be a *prophetic* record of the career of Jesus as much as the New Testament was a *retrospective* one. The first Christian "testament" was employed in this project equally with the second. Much of this work of identifying the meaning of Jesus' death has been done, as numerous histories of Christian doctrine disclose. Some of these are tendentious, as one would expect. Of particular note, we will see how, in those first centuries, early Christian writers came fatefully to attribute responsibility for Jesus' death to "the Jews."

In sum, I will examine the death of Jesus in itself; in the interpretation of its significance by those who first reckoned it a religious mystery and later by scoffers at such an absurd conceit; in its theological development; and in the pieties, impieties, and perplexities that have always attended it.

1

The Crucifixion of Jesus:
How, Why, and by Whom?

There seems to be little reason to doubt that Jesus of Nazareth died in the way ascribed to him, namely, as the recipient of the Roman sentence of death by crucifixion. Nineteenth- and early twentieth-century denials that he ever existed, popular among some rationalists, or that "Jesus" was simply an ideal figure representing the suffering innocent Jew who embodied every biblical virtue, can no longer be taken seriously.

In 30 C.E., the most reliable death date, Jesus was a young man, probably in his thirties, and presumably healthy. He was likely a small man, as the skeletons of many Semites of the ancient world suggest. The Gospels say that Pontius Pilate, the Roman prefect of Judea, had Jesus scourged before handing him over to be crucified. After this the soldiers clothed him in purple, wove a crown of thorns for him, and mocked him as "King of the Jews" (the Greek is better rendered "King of Judea"). In the Gospel of Mark, probably the first of the four to be written, striking Jesus' head with a reed and spitting on him preceded the mock homage.[1] John has all the scourging and mocking details of Mark but not the spitting.[2] He inserts them as activities of the (Roman) soldiers in the middle of the extended dialogue he composes between Pilate and Jesus at the praetorium or armed garrison (18:28–19:16). The two principals are inside the building; unspecified Judeans, except for "the chief priests and the [temple] guards," are outside in the courtyard. At the end of the inserted material that constitutes the lengthy dialogue, they respond to Pilate's invitation, "Behold, the man!" with the outcry, uttered twice, "Crucify him" (John 19:6).

The Markan passion narrative, as it is called, has little detail beyond what is contained in the third of the three predictions of Jesus' death placed on his lips: "The Son of man will be handed over to the chief priests and the scribes, and they will condemn him to death and hand him over to the Gentiles, who will mock him, spit upon him, scourge him, and put him to death, but after three days he will rise."[3] No eyewitness testimony to Jesus' movements on his last day alive need have been required for the Gospel report of occurrences that led up to

his death. The knowledge that he died by crucifixion would have been enough. The evangelists probably did not know which soldiery,
Roman or Jewish, visited what cruelties on
Jesus, although those on whose reminiscences
they drew may have known. The writers of the
Gospels possessed the general remembrance
that temple and imperial armed forces had
acted on orders, the first to harass, then the latter to execute Jesus. That would be all they
would need to know in order to tell of Herod
Antipas and Pilate, mutual antagonists brought
together briefly over a common enemy. For,
whatever Jesus' alleged crimes, he was at least
guilty of having infused hope of political lib-
erty in an oppressed populace, a fact that would
have posed a threat to the occupying power and
its priestly collaborators. Pilate's death sentence is reported as delivered reluctantly, but it
was he alone who delivered it. The Gospel writers chose to feature the temple priesthood's ini-
tiation of the action against Jesus rather than
its final execution, for reasons that need to be
explored.

Crucifixion in the Ancient World

The origins of crucifixion are hard to trace. Not
only Jews but Greeks, Romans, and those that
both of them denoted barbarians considered it
an obscene form of punishment. It is commonly
called Persian or Medean in its origins, proba-

bly because Herodotus (d. after 430 B.C.E. frequently has these peoples employing it.[4] From Herodotus it is impossible to be sure whether impaling corpses on a stake or hanging the condemned up to die is in question. Again, whether the victims were affixed by nails or lashed with thongs is not clear in individual citations, any more than whether an upright stake alone or a crossbeam also was used. The only detailed account of a crucifixion Herodotus supplies is the administration of the punishment by the Athenian general Xanthippus to the satrap Artaÿctes for what are called religious offenses: "They nailed him to planks and hanged him aloft; and as for his son, they stoned him to death before his father's eyes."[5]

Detailed descriptions come only from Roman times. Seneca (d. 65 C.E.) refers to a variety of postures and different kinds of tortures on crosses: some victims are thrust head downward, others have a stake impale their genitals, still others have their arms outstretched on a crossbeam.[6] The Jewish historian Josephus, writing of the Jewish War of the late 60s, is explicit about Jews captured by the Romans who were first flogged, tortured before they died, and then crucified before the city wall. The pity he reports that Titus, father of Josephus's imperial patron Vespasian, felt for them did not keep Titus from letting his troops dispatch as many as five hundred in a day: "The soldiers, out of the rage and hatred they bore the prisoners, nailed those they caught, in different postures, to the crosses for the sport of it, and their number was so great that there was not enough room for the crosses and not enough crosses for the bodies."[7] Josephus calls it "the most wretched of deaths." He tells of the surrender of the fortress Machaerus on the east shore of the Dead Sea when the Romans threatened a Jewish prisoner with crucifixion.[8]

An especially grim description of this punishment, meted out to murderers, highwaymen, and other gross offenders, is the following from a didactic poem: "Punished with limbs outstretched, they see the stake as their fate; they are fastened, nailed to it with sharpest spikes, an ugly meal for birds of prey and grim scraps for dogs."[9]

Much later in Latin speech *"Crux!"* became a curse, to indicate the way the speaker thought the one accursed should end. Other epithets among the lower classes found in the writings of Plautus, Terence, and Petronius are "Crossbar Charlies" (*Patibulatus*) and "Food for Crows" (*Corvorum Cibaria*).[10]

Flogging usually preceded crucifixion among the Romans, as with the Carthaginians. It weakened the victims to such a degree that their time on the cross was shortened.[11] Lashes of a whip are assumed, but sometimes "rods" are mentioned, bringing the torture closer to a cudgeling, depending on their thickness.[12] This was the normal Roman punishment for deserters, later transferred to those guilty of uprising against the state and high treason. The punishment *crux* will be named first among the three most severe, following Cicero's usage of the term for "supreme penalty." Nailing was the commonest form of affixing a body to a tree trunk or crossbar, with lashing by bonds done only in addition.[13] The evidence for a peg or saddle on the stake to support the body at the crotch, thus extending life and torment, is elusive. Seneca says: "You may nail me up and set my seat upon the piercing cross" and speaks of "weighing down upon one's wound"; H. Fulda supplies extensive documentation on the subject.[14] If the victims were generally supported on crosses by such a seat, the custom of leg breaking mentioned in John 19:32-33 would be accounted for. Deprived of the rigidity supplied by the lower limbs, the abdominal cavity would sag, bringing on death by asphyxiation.

The record of history on crucifixion as a torture, with all its ugly refinements, is such that one is led to conclude that Jesus' execution was carried out with relative dispatch. As the Gospels describe it in economical prose, it was a matter of inquiry and sentence shortly after sunrise and death by midafternoon. The torments that preceded Jesus' death are given in much greater detail than the death itself. In John's Gospel the actual crucifixion is described in thirty-six Greek words excluding articles and enclitics (19:17-18), while the account of shooting dice for his garments by soldiers that follows shortly requires fifty-seven (vv. 23-24).

What types of persons were subjected to this cruel ending in the ancient world, and to whom was it seldom or never administered? The short answer to the first is: the slaves and lower classes; soldiers, even in command positions (but not generals); the violently rebellious and the treasonous. As to the second, citizens of the Greek city-states and of the Roman state were usually done away with more briskly, seldom by crucifixion. Poisoning, stabbing, and beheading were the favored methods. But in general the highborn did not die that way. It was considered too cruel and, not least, too demeaning for the upper classes. Administered to any but slaves or those who threatened the existing social order, it would be an admission that the minority citizen class could be capable of such bestial conduct. But philosophers, playwrights, and poets did not engage in any serious attempt to stamp it out. Like American slaveholding in the last century, it was deemed an acceptable social evil.

Josephus was both a Jewish patriot and an apologist for Roman behavior in his Judean homeland. Just before the passage quoted above (in the text at pp. 14–15), he defends Titus by saying that the commander hoped that the gruesome sight of the corpses of those of Jerusalem who attempted flight would move the ones within the walled city to surrender. Josephus's vocabulary is interesting here. The besieged Jerusalemites he describes as common folk among the poor, while those leading the resistance within are rebels or insurgents abetted by brigands outside the city.

Decreeing crucifixion for rebellious Jews was Rome's way of saying that it considered this proud people no better than a slave population.

The Christian Presentation of Jesus' Mode of Death

Minucius Felix was a Christian apologist who wrote a dialogue around 200 C.E. entitled *Octavius*.[15] In it a pagan named Caecilius accuses Christians of every sort of superstition destructive of true religion, including eating babies and copulating randomly in the dark.[16] Another of their follies is the worship of one who has been crucified. They get the kind of altars proper to the abandoned wretches they are because their rites center on a man punished for his crime. He received the direst penalty on the bestial crossbeams of wood.[17] It was a slaves' punishment, the class who most often received it.

The Christian Octavius acknowledges that the mode of Jesus' death was a scandal even for those who first believed in him, but he meets the charge obliquely rather than head on. Omitting any pursuit of the way Jesus met his fate, he says in the apologetic fashion employed by

Hellenistic Jews in the wisdom literature of the Bible that the pagans do worse by venerating wooden gods. They hold in honor signs of victory such as banners and standards that are cruciform and made of wood; perhaps the wood of the god of their worship was even at one time "part of a gallows"![18] Important here is the avoidance of the real problem, the death of one who claimed to be God's own Son on a tree of "shame." Cicero (d. 43 B.C.E.) called crucifixion "the most horrendous torture."[19] Small wonder that in Minucius Felix's treatise, written almost two centuries after the fact, calculated to persuade pagans that the one God of the Christians was the God of the philosophers, the author should sidestep the criminal's death that Jesus died, a man for whom divine honors were being claimed.

The earliest believers in Jesus had no such hesitancy in referring to his crucifixion. Indeed, they made a special point of his shameful ending. Jesus' earliest followers, all of them Jews, proclaimed this tortured death among Jews, who might have been open to a particular tale of cruelty at the hands of the Roman oppressor. But Jesus' crucifixion was never presented on those terms. If anything, Roman responsibility was de-emphasized in favor of Jewish. Was there, perhaps, some biblical symbolism attached to a death in this fashion that the prophet Jesus was seen to fulfill? There is myriad evidence of God's concern for the suffering just one in Israel (including Joseph thrown into a cistern, Gen. 37:24; Elijah harassed by Ahab and Jezebel, 1 Kings 16–19; and Jeremiah flogged and put in stocks, Jer. 20:2). But as to death by crucifixion, the scanty biblical evidence goes in quite the opposite direction. In a chapter of Deuteronomy that deals variously with expiatory rites over the corpse in an unsolved murder, marriage to women taken captive in war, the rights of the firstborn son even if borne by a despised wife, and the capital charge against an incorrigible son, this passage occurs:

> If a man guilty of a capital offense is put to death and his corpse hung on a tree, it shall not remain on the tree overnight. You shall bury it the same day; otherwise, since God's curse rests on him who hangs on a tree, you will defile the land which the LORD, your God, is giving you as your inheritance.[20] (Deut 21:22-23)

This biblical sanction against allowing a corpse to hang more than one day, together with the accursed state of the one so hung (whatever exactly that meant), probably mirrors and at the same time accounts for the failure of Jews to employ this cruel form of torture. The resort to crucifixion among them for high treason in the Hasmonean period and a puzzling exception of its use in the Mishnah (ca. 180 C.E.) will be dealt with below. But, for the moment, one can see why the claim for a messiah who was crucified would be thoroughly repulsive to the Jewish ear. Paul calls the cross a scandal (commonly translated "stumbling block") to Jews and an absurdity to Gentiles. He does this in writing to the once pagan but now believing communities of Corinth (1 Cor. 1:23) and the highlands of the province of Galatia (Gal. 5:11). Paul makes capital of Jesus' presumably accursed condition in the latter epistle by posing the paradox that his "becoming a curse for us" extended "the blessing of Abraham to the Gentiles through Christ Jesus."[21] One might have expected the earliest believers in Jesus to avoid or at least soft-pedal the fact that Jesus died as a convicted felon.

They did quite otherwise. They wrote at length not simply that it happened and hence was bound to be remembered, but they identified this unqualified evil as somehow a good. Christian apologists like Lactantius (d. ca. 320) and Arnobius (d. ca. 330) would puzzle over why God had not proposed an honorable kind of death for Jesus, but there it was. He died on what the ancient world invariably called in Greek the "criminal wood," as also later in Latin. The Epistle to the Hebrews unblinkingly calls the cross a sign of "shame," saying that Jesus endured it for the sake of the joy that lay before him.[22]

The Roman Crucifixion of Jesus and the New Testament

Two conclusions follow from the above facts as they apply to Jesus of Nazareth. One is that Pilate must have become convinced, perhaps in very short order, that Jesus and the two men crucified with him constituted a serious threat to the peace of the empire. The other is that there is little likelihood that Jesus' disputes with other religious teachers, or even the charge that he spoke blasphemously, was the immediate cause of his death. The fears that the temple priests had of his influence over the populace were reductively political, since the power over the people they feared to lose was a matter of tithes and taxes, not a religious influence or one of spirit. They knew they could count on a swift reprisal by Roman authority if they only couched their account of the "plot" of Jesus and his followers in the right terms.

If any of this theorizing is true, it is hard to know why those Jews who first proclaimed him Israel's crucified and risen Messiah, his disciples in his lifetime, did not appeal to Jewish sympathy for him as one more victim of the Roman state. The Jewish populace knew the empire's multitudinous cruelties all too well. So far as we know, Jesus' disciples never made such an appeal—even though Jewish sympathy for him on these grounds would have been overwhelming. Why did his followers go another route and name as the reasons for his death the jealousy of the learned class and the plotting of the hated priesthood, which had to make its point with the Gentile oppressor if he were to be eliminated? Or did they?

The possibilities, here again, are two: that the Gospels and the book of Acts do not present responsibility for Jesus' death as it was conveyed primitively, by oral accounts in the Aramaic language; or that they do, but that the hatred of the common folk for the high priesthood, which acted as Rome's fiscal agent against them, was even greater than for the ultimate oppressor, distant Rome. It needs to be repeated that Jewish familiarity with crucifixion as a Roman punishment was so intimate and detailed that the muted report of Jesus' subjection to it in the New Testament is a mystery. Did the claim of many associates to have seen him risen from the dead relativize the ignominy of the execution utterly? Or were other, stronger forces at work, such as theological reflection, to put a quite different interpretation on the death than ordinary recollection and resentment would have done? All this we need to speculate on from the scanty data that the New Testament provides.

Did the Jews Crucify?

Before moving to the problems provided by the Gospel accounts of Jesus' appearance before

Jewish and Roman authority, one must attend to a final question concerning crucifixion: Did Jews of the first centuries B.C.E. and C.E. ever themselves resort to this form of capital punishment? If they did not, Pilate's reported statement in John's Gospel at 19:6 is an absurdity. There he is quoted as saying: "Take him yourselves and crucify him. I find no guilt in him." Mark and Matthew have Pilate "delivering Jesus over to be crucified," presumably to the Roman legionaries, but Luke is ambiguous. He speaks of Pilate as summoning "the chief priests, the rulers, and the people" (23:13); and, after telling them he finds Jesus guilty of no capital crime and proposing a flogging to placate them, he "handed Jesus over to them to deal with as they wished" (vv. 22, 25). What "them" does Luke have in mind?

Not much is known about how Roman justice was administered in the provinces, so it is unwise to pronounce on what could or could not have happened. But is there any evidence that Jews, who had so often been the victims of crucifixion, ever administered it?

Josephus reports of Alexander Jannaeus (104–78 B.C.E.) that he crucified eight hundred Jewish allies of Demetrius III, king of Syria, who took up arms against him.[23] Yigael Yadin maintains that the Qumran commentary on Nahum 2:12-14 from Cave 4 and the Temple Scroll refer to this incident when they speak of the punishment for an informer or traitor and for one who deserts his people for the Gentiles.[24] The punishment is being hanged on a tree to die. Traditional talmudic wisdom is that any reference to this mode of torture goes in the other direction, interpreting Deuteronomy 21:22-23 to mean that a criminal is first put to death and then his corpse hanged.[25] Yadin thinks that the twice-occurring phrase "you shall hang him [the traitor; the one who curses his people] on a tree and he shall die" means that the victim shall die as a result of the hanging. He reconstructs the corrupt phrase of the text, "from of old," to read *"thus was it done from of old."* The actions of a Jewish tyrant are not, of course, to be thought of as normal Jewish practice. The question for the moment is: Did it ever routinely happen? Interestingly, Josephus does not report Herod the Great as having carried out any crucifixions.

Extremely puzzling is the mishnaic passage (late second century C.E.) which says that on one occasion Simeon ben Shetah hanged eighty women in Ashkelon, the only city in Palestine the Hasmoneans did not sack.[26] It goes on to report that the sages opposed the hanging of women and that only the blasphemer and the idolater were hanged. Then comes the traditional Jewish understanding.

> How did they hang a man? They put a
> beam into the ground and a piece of wood
> jutted from it. The two hands [of the body]

> were brought together and [in this fashion]
> it was hanged. Rabbi Jose says: The beam
> was made to lean against a wall and one
> hanged the corpse on it as butchers do.[27]

"All that have been stoned must be hanged,"
the same passage says. There is an elaborate description of how the huge stone is to be
dropped from twice the height of a man; if the
first has failed to kill, the stone is dropped a
second time as the victim lies supine. Whether
this form of execution was a memory of ancient
practice at the time of the writing more than it
was a current reality is hard to say. Our present
interest, however, centers on the Jewish technique of hanging the victim after death rather
than before: "A man is hanged with his back to
the gallows and a woman with her face toward
the gallows."[28] This cannot be the *stipes* or the
upright stake in the ground but must be either
the *furca,* a V-shaped rack for carts when it was
not used for this ugly purpose, or the infamous
tau, the crossbeam on a stake in the form of a
T. Yadin thinks the latter type of cross is at-
tested by the iron spike found in a man's heels,
which were nailed together and he hanged
alive, upside down, with his knees over the
crossbar.[29]

In light of the lateness and uniqueness of the
testimony to hanging (crucifixion?) in the
Mishnah, it is improbable that this mode of dis-
play (execution?) had any currency in Jewish

life as a legal punishment. What an incited Jewish mob might have resorted to is impossible to say. In the absence of any Jewish evidence that Jews were regularly inflicting a punishment that had so often been inflicted on them, or any Gospel evidence that a Roman prefect had turned his power of capital sentence over to them in a case of sedition—the charge the Gospel of Luke implies the priesthood brought against Jesus (23:1)—it makes no sense to say that the Jewish authorities crucified him. If that was the way he ended, Roman power must have done it. As to Pilate's taunt in John's Gospel (19:6), if it is historical it need not have been uttered in sarcasm but perhaps in ignorance of Jewish legal custom. He would simply have been giving the implied permission, "If you have some religious reason to eliminate him, go ahead." Pilate would then have indicated Rome's way of doing things on a civil charge, namely, crucifying.

It is more likely, however, that the phrase on Pilate's lips was a calculated Johannine irony. This evangelist frequently has the characters in his drama say more or other than they realize. He makes then unconscious speakers of the truth. If this is the case here, Pilate is telling the priestly inciters to do what they cannot do because of the inhibition of Mosaic precept but what in fact they manage to achieve: Jesus' death by crucifixion.

The Problem of 1 Thessalonians 2:14b-16

Paul speaks often of the death of Jesus (Rom. 5:10; 6:3), at times using the shorthand term "cross" (1 Cor. 1:17, 18; Phil. 2:8; Gal. 5:11; 6:12). Once only does he assign responsibility for it and then it is to the people of Judea, not to Rome. This occurs in the first-written (probably in 50) of his extant letters, 1 Thessalonians, at 2:14b-16. Paul is exhorting the believers in Christ in that large Macedonian city, whom he describes as former idol worshipers (1:9), to persevere in faith despite harassment from their "fellow countrymen" (2:14). The pertinent passage follows:

> For you suffer the same things from your own fellow countrymen as they did from the Judeans [*Ioudaiōn*, related to the quality of Christian faith in *Ioudaia*, which Paul commends, earlier in the verse], who killed both the Lord Jesus and the prophets and persecuted us; they do not please God, and are opposed to everyone, trying to prevent us from addressing the pagans that they may be saved, unto the constant filling up of the measure of their sins. But the wrath of God will come upon them at the end [or, has come upon them at last; the verb is aorist, i.e., timeless].

It has been argued since the mid-nineteenth century that vv. 14-16 in whole or part were an addition to Paul's text by a later, probably Gentile hand.[30] The sentiment provides an uncommonly bitter ending for the prayer of thanksgiving to God that begins at v. 13 (flanked by those of 1:2-10 and 3:9-13). More than that, Paul nowhere else attributes the death of Jesus to anyone, although he often indicates the antipathy of some fellow Jews to his preaching, both those who believe in Jesus and those who do not. Whether the passage is authentic is perhaps less important than the occurrence of a phrase in this piece of occasional correspondence written twenty years after Jesus' crucifixion that takes for granted the recipients' conviction that God has "destined us . . . to gain salvation through our Lord Jesus Christ, who died for us" (5:9–10a). That shows not simply that Jesus' death was to the forefront of Paul's thoughts when he first brought the gospel to Thessalonica but that he had spoken of it as an event that achieved salvation (i.e., deliverance from God's wrath on the last day). A theology of redemption based on Jesus' death, without the details that surrounded it, was already in place. The doubtful character of those verses disputed as Paul's stems not from his incapacity to resort to the apocalyptic language of end-time expectation but from his not having his own Jewish people or the Jews of Judea as a target in his other extant letters.

The Development of the Passion Narratives

What kind of literature are the Gospels, and how historical reliable are they? The range of opinions goes from that of those Christians who hold it as a dogma (a word they would not use) that the divine inspiration of these writings assures the believer that no detail reported by an evangelist can have happened otherwise than as described, to the view of equally devout believers who think that the evangelists possessed few facts about Jesus' last hours besides knowing that Pontius Pilate, encouraged by the antipathy of the temple priesthood, condemned him to be crucified at Passover time because he constituted a threat to the Roman state.

Acting as a narrator or storyteller, the important thing the evangelist had to do was choose from among the materials available and arrange them creatively in such a way as to produce the maximum impact on the hearer. Each Gospel writer was above all an author, not simply a collector, compiler, or editor. We have four works of literature by writers of genius who possessed hundreds of sayings, anecdotes, and tales that they wove into four quite distinct narratives, fresh compositions. They addressed themselves to hearers who already believed in Jesus of Nazareth—that he was mighty in word and work; that he had proclaimed the word of God from Israel's Scriptures as a restorer of Israel's faith in all its pristine power; and that his was a special view to the final consummation of God's world in an age to come.

The Historical Core of Jesus' Last Hours and the Gospels

Jesus had engaged in many disputes with the learned, earning thereby the enmity of some, but such was not his downfall. His religious opinions clearly fell within the allowable limits of dispute in the Israel of his day. The opposition of the power class in Jerusalem is what brought about his dissolution. The high priest at the time, Caiaphas, and his power broker father-in-law, Annas, who were heartily despised by the people as agents of the Caesars acting through the prefects, seem to have brought on Jesus' execution. Jesus evidently consistently spoke against the temple: not the institution of blood sacrifice, any more than the prophets had done, but its perversion by irreligious men who worshiped chiefly at the shrine of their continued exercise of power. The Gospel evidence is that it was they who managed to silence him by playing on the fears of a cruel Roman functionary that he might have a potential uprising on his hands.

It is possible that the hard core of reminiscence about Jesus' last day or days that survived is contained in the succinct summary of Luke 23:1:

> Then the whole assembly of them arose
> and brought him before Pilate. They
> brought charges against him, saying, "We
> found this man leading our people astray;
> he opposed the payment of taxes to Cae-
> sar and maintains that he is the Messiah,
> a king."

All the remaining details in the Gospels could
have been elaborations of that remembered
fact. Even as it stands, the statement is an in-
terweaving of the theological and the political.
"Leading astray" had the religious connotation
for Jews of deceiving the people over the ab-
solute oneness of God. It could also have over-
tones of sedition on the lips of Jewish men of
power who opposed revolt. The opposition to
paying taxes to the occupying power was a
clear distortion of Jesus' watchword on the ab-
solute claim of God over the human, a power
that he nonetheless acknowledged.[31] The charge
that Jesus declared himself Israel's king of the
final age—something the first layer of Gospel
material says he took pains to avoid—could
only have been heard by Roman ears as the
seizure of power that several predecessors of
Jesus ("messianic pretenders") had made it. On
balance, it seems correct to maintain that the
disciples of Jesus after his resurrection reconstructed the events of that Friday on the basis
of the fact that Roman justice disposed of him,
after successful priestly efforts to counter his

mounting popularity by denouncing him with a charge of sedition.

That means that each evangelist culminated his narrative with a reconstructed account of Jesus' apprehension by military power, a Jewish hearing,[32] a Roman trial, and the normal cruelties that accompanied crucifixion. Eyewitness testimony to Jesus' successive adventures on the way to death would have had to be that of the women at the cross because of the Gospels' insistence that his male disciples, but for one anonymous one, were nowhere on the scene after the arrest in the garden. The Cyrenean native drafted into service, Simon, would be another exception (Mark 15:21). Peter's threefold denial that he knew Jesus, like the disciples' flight, is probably authentic reminiscence, on the theory that nothing so damaging to the early leadership would have been passed along if it were not regrettably true.

Basic Elements of the Gospels' Passion Narratives

Mark has as a major theme the necessity under which followers of Jesus labor to suffer as he did despite injustices if they are to have any part in his victory over death. Peter is proposed as the cautionary example of a trust betrayed (Judas too, 14:10-11, 43-46). Mark's lesson to his contemporaries is that no tree in the forest is so tall that it cannot fall, no friendship with

Jesus so assured that it cannot be betrayed. For purposes of fulfilling Jesus' prophecy of the cock's crowing twice to signal the betrayal (14:30), Mark needs to have the denials occur some time before dawn, when cocks crow. But for purposes of juxtaposing the conduct of Jesus' enemies with that of his false friend, the chief priests and the entire Sanhedrin have to be meeting at night too. This interpolation technique of storytelling has resulted in the so-called night trial of Jesus before Jewish authority. Mark remedied the situation somewhat by having the Sanhedrin "convene" (or "take counsel") early the next morning (15:1), having had them judge him deserving of death the night before (14:64).

Matthew, however, who follows Mark carefully without at times recognizing the way Mark is framing his narrative, has the arresting party lead Jesus from Gethsemane directly to where Caiaphas and the scribes and elders are assembled (Matt. 26:57). John does the same, compounding matters by doing as Mark does but adding an Annas-to-Caiaphas move to the nighttime story (John 18:24 in the middle of the sequence 18:15-27). Luke seems alerted to the improbability of an assembly of the Sanhedrin by night and solves it by having Jesus led to the high priest's house for custody, where the denials take place by firelight and the guards torment Jesus (Luke 22:54-65). He is brought before the Sanhedrin only "when day came" (v. 66). Despite these correctives, the memory of a judgment of condemnation by the highest body in Israel in totally illegal circumstances has been firmly fixed in Christian memory. By the second century in the Greco-Roman world these believers were interpreting symbolic narrative as history. They had lost the Semitic skill of spotting a story crafted in biblical style. Christians have been misreading their own holy books ever since, often making Jews pay the price of their incomprehension.

The account of the trial of Jesus by Pilate in John will serve as a second example of dramatic narrative that has become confused with mere fact (John 18:28–19:22). Using the irony of which he is supremely capable, this evangelist takes the cause of Jesus' crucifixion placarded above his head and explores it from the standpoint of faith in him versus the unfaith of "the world." In John the placard (*titlos*—a term with which the ancient world's accounts of crucifixions are familiar) reads "Jesus the Nazorean, the king of Judea" (19:19).[33] Only John tells of its wording in Hebrew, Latin, and Greek and of Pilate's adamantine stand against changing it to read that Jesus claimed to be such. Whatever the significance of the title in the minds of the executioners—and its recording in all four Gospels says something about its authenticity—John decides to make capital of it with an essay in drama form on authority as confused with coercive power. Jesus has

supreme authority under God and in that sense
is a king. He is summoned for judgment—and
himself passes judgment on his judge. None of
Jesus' disciples is likely to have witnessed such
a colloquy (despite John's claim at 18:15 that
"the other disciple" than Peter was known to
the high priest). It is a pure construct, a tidy
playlet: one of numerous such in this Gospel.
John is theologizing the scanty history he pos-
sesses and means to do so.

The other evangelists do the same, if not so
overtly. They have a story to tell of a huge injustice wrought against a supremely just one
who is just with the justice of God. They know
who the characters in their story are, real and
perhaps devised. Barabbas (lit., "son of the father," a name unknown in Jewish usage) may
be one of the latter. He is portrayed as the
guilty insurrectionist set free while the innocent Jesus dies on the same charge. The centu-
rion of Mark 15:39 who pierced Jesus' side
with his lance may be another. Mark needed
someone for plot purposes to give testimony at
the end that Jesus was indeed Son of God. He
chose a pagan to give Jesus the coup de grâce
while at the same time uttering a statement of
faith.

Four different authors wrote four passion
plays, each one employing his play as penulti-
mate in the career of Jesus. The last act of the
play is Jesus' having risen from the dead. All
but Mark provide a series of appearances of

Jesus to his friends, in a context of faith in him
as risen.

As Mark tells his story "the Pharisees with
the Herodians" mount a plot against Jesus early
in his public career (3:6). While the house of
Herod had lost power in Judea in 6 C.E. with the
displacement of Archelaus, son of Herod the
Great, by a succession of Roman prefects beginning with Coponius, Herod Antipas still
ruled in Jesus' home province of Galilee and in
Perea partly across the Jordan. There is no
telling the resentment and scheming of the politically disaffected hangers-on of the house of
Herod, but Mark puts them in strange company
with the Pharisees. Those purists about law observance had religious interests from which the
political were never absent.[34] Their opposition
to Jesus, however, found early in Mark, sur-
vives in all four Gospels in the form chiefly of
his debates with the learned. The first three
Gospels call these observants "the scribes and
the Pharisees" or something similar, while for
John they are "the Judeans" or "Jews" (a term
with hostile connotations in 37 of its 71 occurrences) or "Pharisees."

This terminology creates the problem of
whether Jesus went to his death as a result of
incurring the hatred of the Jewish observant
and learned class. The polemic he is reported
engaging in, most bitterly in John but also in
the first three Gospels, might lead one to think
so. In fact, his claim to forgive sins in his own

name and the titles "Messiah" and "Son of the Blessed" acknowledged by him and "Son of man" put on his lips as early as the writing of Mark (14:61-62) result in the charge of blasphemy (v. 64). By a Torah standard, he was never guilty of blasphemy in any recorded utterance. In fact, as has been said, none of the interpretations of the law attributed to him in the Gospels falls outside the range of acceptable rabbinic opinions from whatever we can know of them in his time. Most of the data on the question are from a later date. In brief, nothing in the Gospel record leads up to a charge of blasphemy for claiming any of the prerogatives of God, let alone full equality with God. Yet the Gospels leave the distinct impression that his teaching led to threatening opposition to him which culminated in his execution. If the punishment of crucifixion was as harsh as the pagan accounts of it indicate, what could Jesus be thought to have done to send him to such an ignominious death?

A Tentative Judgment on Motives

What led to Jesus' death can only lie in the fear of Pilate that Jesus was spearheading a movement of the liberation of Jews from Roman rule. He was perfectly justified in such suspicions. He may have witnessed mass demonstrations in Jesus' favor in the few short days before his attention was brought to Jesus as the potential leader of an uprising. Something, someone, convinced Pilate that Jesus was so dangerous that he had to go to the stake. If he was perceived as a threat to Jewish power as well as to Roman power, as seems to be the case, the two in concert would have wished to eliminate him. A temple priesthood fearful that a Jew was acting against the empire: that was the perfect formula for moving against one whose chief threat was to the twofold industry of temple sacrifice and collusion over collecting taxes.

If there is anything to these speculations, why did not the evangelists express the cause of Jesus' death more straightforwardly? Why did they leave future generations to work it out as a historical puzzle? Some say that the Gospel writers adopted an apologetic stance, trying to protect their infant communities against Roman reprisal, in memory viewing the temple and its priests as a paper tiger, now that it was destroyed. But against this view is the total disregard of Roman sensibilities represented by Jesus' contemptuous treatment of Pilate in John. The serious apologist before the empire would never have let that pass.

A much more likely explanation is that all sorts of polemical exchange over what it meant to be an observant Jew had taken place in the diaspora, where the Gospels were written, after the Gentiles sacked Jerusalem. This argumentation is probably much more reflected in the

Gospels than any that took place in Jesus' lifetime. Believers in his resurrection had had fifty
years or more to make claims for his status vis-
à-vis the God of Israel. The Johannine community was making claims of his full possession of
deity.

This would tend to put religious questions in
the foreground and historical, political ones in
the background. The Gospels were written not
as works of history but as existential documents of faith for their time. Engagement with
the civil powers or with the now powerless
temple priesthood would have been part of fad-
ing memory.

When all the problems that attend the Gospel
accounts of Jesus' sentencing to death have
been faced, one major one remains. It is not
whether the Jewish authorities crucified him on
a count of blasphemy (they almost certainly
had the power to execute on a religious charge,
but they did not crucify) or why the historical
traditions that developed theologically into the
four Gospel accounts ended in a deemphasis on
Roman responsibility and an emphasis on
priestly complicity. No, the main problem is
what convinced Pilate that this teacher, of
whom perhaps he had never heard, should be
eliminated in the company of two nameless
others, without any follow-up made to appre-
hend his companions. Why submit Jesus to a
torture reserved for slaves, highwaymen, trai-
tors, and plotters or active insurgents without

tracking down the plot of which he was a part? Since Jesus clearly fell into none of the first three categories, what could have convinced Pilate that he belonged in the fourth? Jesus' punishment seems wildly disproportionate to his crime, even if it were only an alleged crime.

One possibility that the earliest believers in Jesus could not have known of, hence not reported on, is that his popularity with crowds especially in Galilee had caused him to be under Roman surveillance for some time. This could result in picking him off as the leader of a movement at the optimum time, namely, the chief pilgrimage feast, as a way to dissuade all Jews from entertaining any ideas of revolt. Such a hypothesis would further mean that the earliest traditions the evangelists inherited were quite wrong in speculating that the temple priests had a leading part in the affair. The priesthood may have had no part or only a minor one.

Another possibility is that Jesus was condemned to death by a suspicious Roman functionary in a case of mistaken identity. The suggestion is not so absurd as it sounds. His crucifixion as one of three to die in this way invites it. Many an innocent person has been put to death after a court process that took the alleged criminal for someone else.

Crediting the Gospels with a more accurate memory of the basic facts, the major remaining possibilities are two: that Jesus' entry into the city had been hailed by a handful of admirers of his deeds amidst a larger crowd of Galileans, who settled on him as representing their liberationist cause. The other possibility is the one the Gospels hint at most strongly: the judicial council of seventy(-two?) over which the high priest presided took the initial steps to be rid of Jesus because his anti-temple declarations and behavior were taken to be an attack on the religion of Israel itself. The council engineered Jesus' death by using the prefect Pilate as their unwitting tool, this man who normally manipulated others. Both centers of power had the overwhelming will to stay in power, the one political, the other religio-political. Such people make hasty alliances and act harshly to put down any perceived threat. The clearest memory that the earliest believers in Jesus had—however devoid they were of hard facts—was that throne and altar had acted together against a common enemy: not so much Jesus' person as Jesus as the cause of a possible change in the temple priesthood's fortunes. He only represented it. It would have been Pilate's discovery that Jesus aspired to kingship on terms he did not comprehend that would have settled the matter in his mind.

How Mark's Trial and Passion Account Was Framed

A reconstruction that does no violence to the kind of writing the Gospels are might go as fol-

lows. The believers in Jesus' resurrection retained the basic memory that he had been executed brutally amidst the hubbub of a
pilgrimage feast. The city had been crowded to
overflowing; the temple traffic in commerce
was carefully controlled as always; there were
lost children everywhere. A diversion outside
the city walls was promised: some criminals, in
Jewish parlance, "hung up alive" (there was no
word in their language for "crucify" or "crucifixion"). Who were the condemned and what
had they done? There was little solid information on this point. There never was. The question of who was responsible was not raised. For
an oppressed people there is only one answer—
the government or the army, which come to the
same thing. Those who witnessed the gruesome
show would have been either angry or silently
admiring, depending on where they stood on
the condemned men or on Roman "justice."
Most onlookers had no way of telling if the victims were plunderers of the poor or patriots.
There would have been rumors about the
charge against them but nothing confirmable
on the spot: the placards over the victims'
heads were often lies, and one was utterly cryp-
tic, "Jesus of Nazareth, King of Judea."

So many were disposed of in this way. But
on the occasion of the feast! Had the pagans no
sense of the "piety" they kept boasting of as a
Roman virtue? The word might have spread
among the crowd looking on in guilty horror:
"One of them is different, the just one from the

north. We have heard stories of his teaching and his deeds. Why would they want to kill *him*?"

"That is just the kind they can't stand," the answer might have come. "He reminds them of the rotten show they are running. The Romans, the temple priests. It's all the same crowd." But others might have said: "He threatened to destroy the temple of the LORD; I heard him say it."

Those who heard the initial "witnesses to the resurrection" proclaim Jesus as crucified and risen—and that became the technical term for the large apostolic company to whom Jesus appeared in his new, altered state (Acts 1:22)—would have heard Jesus' death always referred to as something God allowed to overtake him. Questions like, "Could any Jews have sought the destruction of a fellow Jew under the occupation?" or "Was it not the pagans who finished him off in their fashion?" do not seem to have arisen in the Christian circles whose record we have. That either the temple priesthood or the Roman prefect was capable of ruthless action they would have taken for granted. The earliest promulgation of Jesus' death and resurrection was almost certainly as a deed of God, given the absence of any details in the earliest extant proclamation. It was told in the form in which it appears in Paul's first letter to Corinth (15:3) as "what was handed on." He transmitted it roughly a quarter century after the event in this unadorned phrase: "that Christ died for our sins in accordance with the scriptures." Paul at the same time reminded his congregation of former pagans and a few Jews that he had thus first presented it.

This word about Jesus' death in the Jewish diaspora was given no apologetic cast. It did not assign blame; it was not even described as an execution. The message was probably conveyed to an entire first generation of believers in this form, both within and outside Palestine. In the homeland, however, details would have been ferreted out by Jesus' friends whose belief in his resurrection had rehabilitated them from the shame of their abandonment of him. These fragments of remembrance may or may not have taken the form of a sequential narrative. The memory of the previous night in Gethsemane would, of course, have remained. So would that of Peter's denying that he knew Jesus, of Jesus' having appeared before some arm of Jewish justice, and of the Roman arraignment that sealed his fate. None of these reminiscences can be assumed to have been transmitted in their bald, factual condition. As they reach us in the Gospels they are laced through with typologies, that is, the fulfillment of biblical "types" or figures in Jesus, the perfect antitype. The Hebrew Scriptures employ this internal technique frequently. It seems to have marked the earliest form in which the account of Jesus' sufferings and death was passed along.

There would have been this elaboration from the start, as is the case in ancient historiography generally when facts are in short supply and there is deep commitment to a person or cause. The basic facts were never in doubt: arrest by Roman soldiery or the temple police (a fully paramilitary force) or both; detention and questioning by the temple priesthood, magnified in the telling to the full Sanhedrin; an appearance before the Roman prefect Pilate; and sentence to death on a charge of sedition.

When these fragments were first woven into a story is not known. The material is Palestinian. It is impossible to tell if there first emerged an Aramaic narrative or a Greek one from multiple, Aramaic-derived Greek sources. Many maintain that the first evangelist to write, Mark, constructed the first trial and passion story. Others say he had one at hand that he edited. Another puzzle is what additional sources, if any, Luke and John had.

Looking more closely at Mark, we find Jesus entering Jerusalem as a pilgrim accompanied by shouts of popular acclaim. It was traditional Jewish practice to recite Psalm 118 to welcome new arrivals (v. 26; cf. Mark 11:9b). Adding to it a phrase from the dynastic oracle of 2 Samuel was not traditional. Only a pre- or post-Easter conviction that Jesus was Messiah could account for this. In the Markan form it is given as: "Blessed is the kingdom of our father David *that is to come*" (Mark 11:10a from 2 Sam.

7:16), with the italicized words a paraphrase of "kingdom . . . and throne that shall stand firm forever." If the reminiscence is authentic, Jesus could be perceived from these shouts to have plans for a political insurgency. David's throne in Judea, after all, was the one the Hasmonean dynasty and the now displaced Herodian house claimed, even though neither derived from David genealogically. No action is reported against Jesus on this occasion, however, despite all the words that swirled about his head.

The next event is a deed that was directed at the heart of the temple, which had as its business blood sacrifice to God (Mark 11:15, 17). Mark plants in the center of Jesus' action against the money changers a reminder of his scruple about an oral precept against defiling the sacred space: "He did not permit anyone to carry anything through the temple area" (v. 16). That later editorial addition was meant to establish Jesus' sensitivity to purity laws, as if to say that his opposition to cultic purity was not in question. The overturning of the tables was unmistakably a symbolic act that constituted an offense against divinity itself in the eyes of the temple's priestly custodians. Mark retained a recollection of this act that looked to the temple's future destruction and restoration. It was known to John from another source (John 2:13-22). The challenge of "the chief priests, the scribes, and the elders" that questioned his authority to do "these things" can refer only to his attack on a daily supply of birds and beasts for sacrifice to be purchased with temple coinage (Mark 11:27-29). The intervening challenges in Mark by Pharisees, Herodians, Sadducees, and scribes (see 12:13, 18, 28) in an echo of Jesus' differences with the communities of learning and his voluntarily forfeited political power that Mark has featured throughout. They would have been at one with the temple priests in the shock and outrage that led to his downfall, although on the basis of different perceptions of Jesus' threat to their power.

The plot of the priests and their learned associates skilled in the law begins at 14:1: "The chief priests and the scribes were seeking a way to arrest him by treachery and put him to death." Mark adds a scruple about fear of a riot if it were attempted in the week of Passover (v. 2). His narrative clue in 3:6, which involves a partial set of the same plotters, Pharisees and Herodians (see also 12:13), is a device preparing the reader for the totality of the known opposition. A series of vignettes interrupts the story of the arrest. It includes Judas's plan to betray, the final supper, and Jesus' prayer in the company of his disciples on the Mount of Olives. Judas's conspiring is with the priests, hence it is they from whom the apprehending party comes (v. 43). It is "the high priest and all the chief priests and elders and scribes" (v. 53) before whom Mark says he is led.

To maintain that John's mention of a battalion and a tribune in the arresting party proves

that it was a Roman operation is not very helpful since John has earlier mentioned Judas as
"getting a band from the chief priests and
guards from the Pharisees" (18:3). One cannot
pick one's villains on the basis of what is inher-
ently probable when the Gospel writers seem to
be reporting on two agencies of violence working in concert. Mark's indefinite "*crowd* with
swords and clubs" (14:43), a noun in which
Matthew (26:47) and Luke (22:47) follow him,
may best cover their and our ignorance of the
event. When, one may ask, was military disci-
pline ever preserved on a mission such as this?

Jesus' Temple Predictions as the Cause of His Undoing

Whatever Mark's sources may have contained
about a Jewish hearing, the challenge to Jesus
about his views of the temple is supported by
two things: his recent demonstration against it
(Mark 11:15-19) and the multiple appearance
of his "temple sayings" in the Gospels and Acts
of the Apostles. These indicate that he had
authored some such predictive and perhaps
threatening utterance as: "So you see this great
edifice? There will not be left a stone upon a
stone that will not come hurtling down" (Mark
13:2; parallels in Matt. 24:2; Luke 21:6).[35]
This was the Jesus whose glorified body became
for believers the new temple, replacing the
old. Jesus' dire prediction was altered to read,
under the influence of his resurrection: "[If you]

destroy this temple, in three days I will raise it up" (John 2:19; parallels in Mark 15:29; Matt. 26:61; in Mark 14:58, "made with hands . . . another not made with hands") and in John 4:21: "The hour is coming when you [Samaritans] will worship the Father neither on this mountain nor in Jerusalem."

Mark in his passion story portrays as liars the witnesses to what Jesus has said (14:57), and their testimony as not agreeing (v. 56). But that is because for Mark Jesus alone is the truth. We surely have in his account the kernel of the Jewish leadership's case against him. Before this they had identified him as prophesying the destruction of the still uncompleted edifice (John 2:20). The faith of the Markan church in Jesus as the Christ and Son of God is put on Jesus' lips when he is questioned (Mark 14:61-62; cf. 1:1). Neither claim—if, as is unlikely, he made both with an affirmative "I am"—nor the prophecy that the Son of man coming with the clouds of heaven will be seated at the right hand of the Power would merit the charge of blasphemy with which the high priest responded. The biblical conditions for blaspheming are not fulfilled either here or in the healing of the paralytic (2:7). Exodus 20:7 gives the basic prohibition against reviling God. (Hebrew has no precise word for "blaspheme" or "blasphemy.") This is followed up by the punishment of the whole community's stoning to death anyone who *curses* the sacred name, YHWH (Lev. 24:11). Em-

ployment of the Name seems essential. Yet Isaiah 37:6 has the commander of the Syrian
troops represent his king in saying that the LORD
will not save Judah, as King Hezekiah maintains
the LORD will do (36:15, 18); the prophet responds by telling the servants of the king that
such an utterance "reviles God."

In the Greek translation of the Old Testament, "blasphemy" fittingly describes any utterance that is taken to threaten God's
uniqueness or majesty.[36] Yet the claim to be
God's son or God's anointed king (Mark 14:61)
would not be taken in Jesus' day to constitute
blasphemy (v. 64). When the high priest asks if
Jesus thinks he is such a one he is told: "I am."
Surely this reflects the polemic in which the
Markan church has been engaged, where this
twofold claim for Jesus is taken to connote
much more and hence is blasphemous in the
wider sense. An encroachment on the divine
majesty is understood by the larger Jewish
community later in the century as it hears the
titles claimed for Jesus (see John 10:33 for an
even greater understanding). Mark's account of
the priestly hearing reflects the decades of
polemic that have gone before.

Would the heated post-resurrection exchange
between Jewish believers in Jesus and Jewish
disbelievers in him be the only explanation
of how "blasphemy" got into Mark's Gospel?
Scarcely. Its wide range of meaning among
Greek-speaking Jews would qualify Jesus' dec-

laration in his lifetime that the temple was
to come down as an attack on the God whose
house it was. Jesus himself rejected swearing
"By heaven!" "By the earth!" and "By Jerusalem!" as thinly veiled avoidances of the divine
name (see Matt. 5:34-35). Surely an attack on
the temple could be construed as an attack on
the person of YHWH. The temple sayings attributed to Jesus in their non-theologized, pre-
Easter form were not the predictions of a man of
foresight that the temple *would* be destroyed.
They were prophetic declarations that God
would bring it down, replacing it with a new
one of the final age. Jesus is not to be placed in
the company of the writing prophets, whom
Christian theologians of recent centuries mis-
takenly classified as promoters of a "purer" religion than one of blood sacrifice. He belongs in
their company as one who foresaw a sacrifice
befitting the final age to replace the one the
high priesthood was presiding over.

Jesus' teaching on proper interpretations of
law observance may have elicited annoyance,
anger, even violent response from teachers who
thought otherwise. It was not such as to bring
on a plot to kill him. A careful comparison of
what he taught with rabbinic teaching of a later
age, critically scrutinized, reveals no major differences, only minor ones of emphasis and
opinion. Yet intimations of the will to eliminate
him are pervasive in the Gospels. They cannot
be traced exclusively to death threats against

his disciples of a later time. Violent exchanges over his anti-temple stance would explain best the survival of these exchanges in the Gospel tradition (see John 8:59; 10:31; 11:53). They are theologized as a result of later christological debates, to be sure, but their primitive form is not hard to identify: "This temple which is God's house will be, should be destroyed." This is not an evangelist of the 60s or 70s C.E. making Jesus a predicter of the future after the event. It is the work of a recorder of his earthly career in a tradition that has never forgotten the utterances of one who threatened destruction of the temple, embarrassing as they may be to record. This would account for the reported threats on his life in a way that his teaching would not, except insofar as his teaching was integral to the prophecy spoken in God's name.

Suspicion of Rebellion?

If Jesus' words and his symbolic deed against the temple were sufficient to arouse the desire of the priests and elders to be rid of him, the empire's suspicion of his complicity in rebellion would even more surely bring about his summoning on charges. Much has been made in recent writing of his associations with revolutionary types such as Judas son of Simon the *Iscariot* (Mark 3:18; John 6:71), taken to be questionably related to the Greek loanword from Latin, *sikarios*, a dagger wielder; his disciple Simon "the Zealot" (Luke

6:15; elsewhere "the Cananaean," Mark 3:18; Matt. 10:4), understood to be a member of a guerilla band; Simon *Baryona* (usually, "son of Jonah," Matt. 16:17), an Aramaic word for bandit or gangster; and the designation for James and John, *Boanērges,* "sons of thunder" (Mark 3:17). The philology is doubtful in three cases and it is by now established that "zealot" meant simply *that* in a religious sense until the late 60s, when it was first attached to bands of insurrectionists.

If the above tags described five of Jesus' companions—the last two given as *his* designation of them—we might have expected the Gospels, having retained this much, to suggest something of their activities. No scrap of anti-Roman action is hinted at. Implicit in some of Jesus' parables, however, is a reminder of the gross injustices under which Jesus' peasant hearers labored. Many of them had lost their land as debtors because of the heavy taxes imposed by Rome and collected by Jewish land agents. The whole fiscal system was ultimately administered by the high priests, but the peasant farmers tended not to know this. They took their wrath out on the large owners or their overseers whose sharecropping tenants they were, land their fathers and grandfathers had forfeited.[37] The distinct possibility exists that Jesus became a popular figure of a quite different sort than he intended, as witnessed by the fragment in John that says he knew "they were going to come and carry him off to make him king" (John 6:15). He is described in the remainder of that verse as having withdrawn again "to the mountain alone," but it is a scene that could have been played out more than once and culminated in the way the crowds hailed him on his entry into Jerusalem.

His constant references to kings and the kingdom in his teaching were to YHWH, Israel's only king, and the full dominion this Sovereign hoped to exercise over all Jewish hearts. No futurist scheme need have been intended: a sway expected by Jesus only at "the end of days." "Kingship" or "reign" was a "now" word in Jesus' intention, and not in John's Gospel only. However religiously he intended it, it would have been heard politically as well. For Jews there was no distinction between the two. Life under their God was for them a totality. If Jesus was a restorationist, and all the Gospel evidence is that he meant to be, he would have spoken of the kingship of YHWH but been heard to mean the kingship of David.

Such being the case with Jewish hearers, how could the following utterance reach the Roman ear without connoting an active seizure of power: "Amen, I say to you, there are some standing here who will not taste death until they see that the kingdom of God has come in power" (Mark 9:1)? Both Jewish and Roman authority would have wondered why large crowds would have gathered in Galilee to hear this man if not with a view to an uprising. This

was not a question put by imperial and Sad-
ducee paranoia alone. It could equally have
been asked by Jewish hope.

It is scarcely believable that the army of occupation, made up of troops from the other
colonies and not legionaries of Rome proper,
had heard nothing of Jesus' popular acceptance.
The question is not, however, What did Pilate
know and when did he know it? It is, What
prompted him to take the act of condemning
Jesus to death that he did? The Gospels provide
an answer, namely, condemnation by a Jewish
court that triggered Jesus' remanding to Roman
justice. Such, at least, is the Mark-Matthew tradition. Luke mutes the Sanhedrin's judgment of
condemnation (see 22:71), and John has the
chief priests handing Jesus over to Pilate (18:35)
but without a clear charge, only that he must be
a malefactor (it is literally a "doer of evil") or
they would not have done it (v. 30).

The Ambiguous Passion Accounts and Their Emergent Theme

It is impossible to conclude from the Gospels
what sequence of events brought Jesus to the
cross. It is likely that the evangelists did not
know it with any precision and opted to place
the blame in a way that is not easy to decipher.
Ambiguity is the hallmark of all four accounts.
What the writers seemed to know was that Jewish and Roman authorities wanted him out of

the way and achieved it in some fashion, concerning which the four had no single clear tradition. The situation is complicated by their conviction that Jesus' death was by no means simply a human drama. God was behind it at every stage, not simply as permitting it but decreeing that it should have ended as it did.

The conventional wisdom has been to maintain that Pilate is portrayed sympathetically and his ultimate responsibility as the hanging judge downplayed for apologetic reasons. The Jesus movement, if not courting imperial favor, was at least trying to avoid political censure. This was especially true of Mark's narrative, the argument goes. He compiled his Gospel in Rome and there played the apologist for his coreligionists. Those who favor this line fail to explain why Mark left so much Roman brutality in his account that he could wisely have omitted, including Pilate's part in the affair. The exchange between Jesus and Pilate in John is completely oblivious to giving offense to Rome. The apologia, if such it was, was evidently not very well carried off. Another consideration regarding this theory is that it assumes that the materials that went into the Gospels were written by and for Gentiles with no attention paid to Jewish sensibilities, only to Roman. Whatever one chooses as the first layer of tradition, however, it contains something to offend everybody, just as the Gospels do in their final form. The evangelists were convinced that a terrible injustice had been done to an innocent man and they were not at pains to protect anyone's sensitivities on that score.

The friends Peter and Judas Iscariot were central figures in the passion narratives, more so than the high priest or Pilate. They, along with Peter's two sleeping companions in Gethsemane and the other male disciples who fled, were presented as examples of infidelity in a time of crisis. Believers in Jesus would have to make similar hard choices between him and the disruption of their lives that fidelity could cause. The women at the cross who looked on from a distance (see Mark 15:40-41; John 19:25-27) are depicted in their persevering love purposefully, even as were the women who did not deliver the message that Jesus had risen, "for they were afraid" (Mark 16:8). The other Gospels portray the latter group as acting quite differently (Matt. 28:8-10; cf. John 20:11-18), likewise for the evangelists' purposes. Thus it is that faulting the Gospel writers for conflicting details as if they had "got it wrong" is to miss what they were up to in getting it right. As modern reporters, they were a flat failure. As ancient dramatists they were quite successful; in assigning human responsibility for Jesus' death, in light of subsequent history they were tragically successful.

Remembering the purposes of the evangelists and their sources, we need to recall first that the conduct of the Roman soldiery and temple guard was of no consequence to them. These men normally acted in brutal fashion and were so depicted. The Sanhedrin, the high priest, and Pilate, similarly, are cardboard figures who act predictably, namely, as functionaries who put the self-serving cause they are dedicated to above justice to an individual.

It is little wonder that the heinousness of the Sanhedrin's action grew in the minds of Jesus' followers. They who should have believed had not, while the Roman prefect, of whom nothing was expected, had been able to ask, "What evil has he done?" (Mark 15:14) and say, "I have found him guilty of no capital crime" (Luke 23:22). The two opposed views of Jesus before his judges were not historical in the ordinary sense. Believers in Jesus probably did not possess enough hard facts for that kind of history writing. They worked up four dramatizations on a biblical model, saying that the enemies of God were of his own people while the despised gentile had acted more nobly. In any event, this emphasis on the part played by the priests and "the whole people" (Matt. 27:25) and the portrayal of Pilate as the vacillating protagonist of Jesus has led to terrible consequences for Jews. It is, however, anachronistic to speak of the "anti-Semitism of the New Testament." "Anti-Judaism" would be a correct second-century term. In the late first century it was the case of a Jewish minority striking out verbally against the Jewish majority for its "anti-Christianism"—

to underscore the absurdity of the other term.
The warfare was between Jewish groups. It is by
now vain to wish it had remained that way.
There are much more bitter statements in the
Dead Sea Scrolls against the Jerusalem temple
priesthood than those found in the Gospels, but
the Qumranites died *as Jews*. The Christian-
Jewish antipathy might have remained one
more example of religion's sorry history of
hurling mutual bans but for the Constantinian
settlement. That changed everything.

Conclusion

Jesus was executed by a Roman punishment
meted out to malefactors of the worst type and
to political insurgents, real or suspected. Pilate's motive for sentencing Jesus, if indeed
Jesus was subjected to a formal trial, is not
known. The highest Jewish religious authority
appears to have been interested in stilling his
voice—exactly why can only be surmised. Neither the four evangelists (nor the book of Acts,
Luke's volume two) nor the sources they drew
on knew what went on when Jesus appeared
before Judean and Roman justice.

How the Jewish court system worked in
Jerusalem at the time is not known; Josephus's
descriptions are conflicting and the much later
Mishnah provides an idealization. The rough
justice of imperial legates in the provinces relative to Roman public law is another unknown.

The tendency of prefects (later "procurators") to use the Jewish pilgrimage feasts as the optimum time for punishing incipient rebellion for exemplary purposes *is* known.

Jesus was a self-declared restorer of the religion of Israel. He did not hesitate to speak of God's plan for the world's final age, in which he and his "twelve" would have a part—he a major one and they a minor. His religious language was that of Israel's future reign and of God's kingship. He spoke and acted against the temple symbolically, saying it would be replaced as part of Israel's restoration. This would have been enough to incur the wrath of the temple priesthood. A fear of sedition in any movement that appeared to have enough strength could account for Pilate's action.

Jesus was probably condemned in as confused circumstances as the ones of which the Gospel narratives seem to have conflicting recollections. They meant to write a theologically interpreted history of the events and ended by writing what was taken for literal history, a history all but impossible to reconstruct with precision, however much individual details can be verified or declared probable.

2

How Jesus' Death Came to Be Seen as Redemptive

The Acts of the Apostles serves as the second volume to match Luke's story of Jesus. Indeed, Paul's summoning before the temple authorities, then two of Pilate's successors, and finally King Agrippa II of Galilee and Perea closely resembles the inquests to which Jesus was subjected (Acts 22–26). The report of Jesus' last hours found in Luke's Gospel is condensed in summaries like the following, with Peter as the speaker:

> You men of Israel, hear these words. Jesus the Nazorean was a man commended to you by God with mighty deeds, wonders and signs, which God worked through him in your midst, as you yourselves know. This man, delivered up by

the design and foreknowledge of God, you killed, using lawless men to crucify him. But God raised him up, releasing him from the throes of death, because it was impossible for him to be held by it. (Acts 2:22-24)

This direct charge to certain men of power in Jerusalem with the death of Jesus, marked by a total lack of nuance, has been highly influential on Christian thinking over the centuries. It identifies as the actual executioners the "lawless" Romans, a term that could either describe their action against an innocent man or designate their paganism (i.e., their status as outside Mosaic law); but the "delivering up" clearly names some Judean Jews as the perpetrators, as Luke's Gospel narrative has made clear (22:66-70; 23:1). Not to be missed is the providential explanation of Jesus' death in Acts 2:23. His death came about, Luke maintains, through God's "design" and "foreknowledge." This identifies the death of Jesus as a deed of God before it is a deed of men.

A second speech of Peter in Acts, also addressed to "You men of Israel," summarizes the version of the dispatching of Jesus in Luke's Gospel more thoroughly:

The God of Abraham, Isaac, and Jacob, the God of our ancestors, has glorified his servant Jesus whom you handed over and

denied in Pilate's presence, when he had
decided to release him. You denied the
holy and just one and asked that a mur-
derer be released to you. The prince [or
"pathfinder"] of life you put to death but
God raised him from the dead. We are
witnesses to this. (Acts 3:12-15)

In still a third passage the Lukan author's uncertainty over who exactly was high priest at
the time (he is unnamed in Luke 22:54) contin-
ues, but he now provides more data. "Their
leaders, elders, and scribes were assembled in
Jerusalem" to question Peter and John about
the healing of a crippled beggar, and teaching
the people, and proclaiming in Jesus the resurrection of the dead (see Acts 3:1-10; 4:2).
Joined to them were "Annas the high priest,
Caiaphas, John, Alexander, and such as were
of the high-priestly class." All these brought
the two disciples into their presence and questioned them. They dismissed Peter and John
after threats, who then reported it, after which
the community prayed: "Indeed, they ['the
Gentiles, the kings of earth, and the princes' of
Ps. 2:1-2] gathered in this city against your
holy servant Jesus, whom you anointed, Herod
and Pontius Pilate, together with the pagans
and the peoples of Israel, to do what your hand
and will had long ago planned should take
place" (Acts 4:5-7, 21, 25-28). Here again the
divine design is paramount, but the multiplica-

tion of human players in the drama tends to obscure this fact.

The written Gospels were composed well after the earliest proclaiming of Jesus as crucified and risen, whatever the first oral forms of the message may have been. When Luke in Acts proposes a basic proclamation of Jesus' death and resurrection (10:34-41), it contains only a fragment of the passion narrative: "They [presumably the people in the region of Judea and Jerusalem of the same verse] put him to death by hanging him on a tree" (v. 39). The demonstrably earlier proclamations of salvation by faith in Jesus' death and resurrection that occur in Paul's letters omit all mention of the historical actors. It is to these that we now turn.

The Crucifixion-Resurrection in Paul's Letters

The problem attending 1 Thessalonians 2:14-16 has been noted in chap. 1 and is referred to below. For Paul's references to Jesus' death (often, "the cross") or resurrection elsewhere in his correspondence, see 1 Thess. 1:10; 4:14; 5:9-10; Gal. 1:4, 2:20-21; 3:13; 6:12-14; Phil. 2:6-11; 1 Cor. 1:13, 18, 23-24; 2:8; 5:7b; 7:23; 8:11, 32; 10:16; 11:26; 15:1-7, 12-17, 20; 2 Cor. 1:5; 4:10; 5:14, 15, 21; Rom. 1:3-4; 3:25-26; 5:6-8; 6:3-4, 9-10; 8:32, 34. These citations show that whenever Paul speaks of Jesus' death or his rising from the dead he has in mind chiefly its effect in the lives of believers ("for us," "for all," "for our sins"). He never refers to either event as a matter of pure history. It is always an occurrence in the contemporary history of the baptized. Paul does not elaborate, moreover, on the circumstances of either death or resurrection except to underscore that in Jesus' dying he suffered.

Paul of Tarsus is often identified by Jews as the Jew they feel most comfortable in despising for his attacks on the law. In fact, the disputed passage from 1 Thessalonians 2 aside ("by the Judeans [or Jews], who killed the Lord Jesus and the prophets and drove us out, and are so heedless of God's will and such enemies of their fellow men" [vv. 14b–15]), Paul bears no responsibility for the sufferings that the Jews of subsequent ages have endured at the hands of Christians for the way he speaks of Jesus' death. His utterances are always in a theological framework devoid of historical details. To read them in their entirety, together with his sole reflection on the lot of his fellow Jews in God's design (Romans 9–11), is to suspect that the invective of 1 Thessalonians is from a later hand.

Paul is the earliest witness we have to the effects the early believers thought Jesus' death and resurrection could achieve in them. He says that the community members in Thessalonica "await God's Son from heaven, whom God raised from the dead, Jesus, who delivers us from the wrath to come" (1 Thess. 1:10). The "wrath" and "deliverance" he speaks of are clearly fragments of Jewish end-time hope.

There are several puzzles here. How could Paul report on the cruel end to Jesus' life in speech so devoid of color and without evident emotion both here and whenever else he refers to it? A person to whom a death means much cannot get so used to its brutal circumstances as never to mention them. It had to be the mythic setting in which Paul had long ago situated this death. The tradition he received and handed on was succinct enough: "that Christ died for our sins in accordance with the scriptures" (1 Cor. 15:3). The center of gravity in the narrative had evidently shifted, some decades before, from the cruel manner of death to the simple fact of death. These events in the life of Jesus did not have their primary importance as regards *him*. They were chiefly important to believers in what God had accomplished through him for *them*. Paul had long ago stopped thinking merely historically, if he ever did so. He was a man of the Bible, and the Bible's only concern with events is what they meant for the lives of the people Israel. So it was with Paul in conjunction with his believing people, whether Jew or Gentile. He saw them as Israel but with an important new, end-time difference, namely, that difference constituted by God's deed in Jesus Christ. He promulgated the fresh reality of the events as a sacred *mythos,* much as the Bible does with the exodus from Egypt.

The Pre-Pauline Tradition: A Redemptive Death

How did the movement that succeeded Jesus interpret his death as expiatory or atoning and do so fairly immediately? There is no evidence that it was interpreted in any other way by believers in Jesus from the beginning than "for our sins." It is true that the experience of Jesus risen from the dead must have radically altered the entire estimate his disciples had of him. Their first thought as they experienced him risen would have been one of vindication by God of this innocent sufferer. Yet such vindication, as they knew it from the Bible, was a matter of hope and far-off expectation. It must have required some little time for them to take in his resurrection, not only the fact but its sudden following upon his death. That fact alone would have relativized his death, put it in a new perspective. But to see it as expiatory, as a matter of supreme benefit to those who would survive him in all ages to come? What could have led to this conviction they held relatively swiftly?

The Jewish idea that a martyr's death is somehow beneficial to others goes back to the late second-century B.C.E. Maccabean revolt. And the daily sacrifice in Jerusalem's temple as expiatory of inadvertent or unconscious sins "put people right with God." A third possibility is the rabbinic familiarity with the "binding of

Isaac" (Genesis 22), the paradigm well known in Jewish circles of God's intervention to rescue the innocent one who was let suffer by God's design. Each of these three examples has been put forward as best accounting for the primitive view of Jesus' death as expiatory.

No primitive Palestinian proclamation of Jews to Jews about Jesus is extant in the Aramaic tongue. One may harbor the suspicion that the entire New Testament was the work of Gentile-oriented Jews beamed at Gentiles on remembered Jewish models, a suspicion that could invalidate its authenticity as a record of Palestinian realities. From the standpoint of critical history, however, it is better to view these writings as containing some authentic recollections of the way Jesus' dying and rising were first presented in Palestine in the 30s. If it were done in any other way, some remembrance should have lingered in the presentation to the Hellenized world reflected in the New Testament. No such alternative set of reminiscences exists. Easier still is it to imagine Paul as having devised a theology of human redemption through faith in the cross and resurrection completely on his own. But this picture of Paul as the inventor of Christianity is based more on animus toward him and a grudging respect for Jesus than on solid critical inquiry into the tradition he received.[1]

Why Call a Crucified Man Israel's Anointed King?

The title of Jesus most closely associated with his given name was "Christ"—not Son of God, Lord, Savior, or any other but the term in Greek for Messiah, God's Anointed.[2] This constitutes a problem. Some early evidence indicates that messiahship is not a role that Jesus courted or claimed (see Mark 8:29, then 6:15 and his ambiguous response, much theologized, when challenged to say plainly if he were the Messiah, John 10:24-30). The title had to do with with the hope for the restoration of Davidic kingship. To be literally of David's house and family was less a messianic qualification than to be victorious in David's mold. Whoever claims to see such ambitions in Jesus is seeing more than the Gospels warrant. The first and early second centuries provide a history of failed messiahs. Their successive defeats, ending in that of Bar Kokhba in Hadrian's time (135 C.E.), proved that the claims made for each of them were premature. Nothing reported of Jesus, *except for the charge on which he died*, namely, "king of the Jews" or "king of Judea," places him in their company. Whoever may have thought of Jesus in such a role—and fragments in the Gospels indicate that some did— had their hopes dashed when he proved to be no winner but a loser by the royal messianic standard then current: military victory.

There was this difference between the popular acclaim he might have received, culminating in his entry into Jerusalem, and that accorded to the series of self-declared leaders of insurgency. He spoke consistently of a new order of the ages, with himself somehow central to it and his companions having a role. A saying common to Matthew (19:28) and Luke (22:30), hence from the hypothetical early collection known as Q, places "the Twelve" on twelve thrones judging the tribes of Israel, with the Son of man seated on his throne of glory. That sort of end-time envisioning is more likely to have originated with Jesus and been remembered than have come to birth as the work of the beleaguered Twelve.

The consistent pattern in the Gospels identifies Jesus' project as the restoration of Israel with him under God as restorer. Those among his own people who opposed him, who are described as turning him over to imperial authority, would have been well alerted to his proclamation of a new order. The dream he harbored, whether it was long-term or short-term in fulfillment, had no place in it for them or for the temple. Every report about him that reached their ears would have confirmed this. His words and actions might well have been thought apocalyptic madness by the Sadducees, who were impatient with all post-Torah speculation. He was in any case taken seriously as a political threat to a sufficient number in the

ruling body known as the Sanhedrin, whatever
its political composition may have been. And
its authoritative voice seems to have prevailed.

This relationship between Jesus as an end-
time figure in his own mind, though not the
Messiah, would seem even more compelling in
triggering opposition to him than his one symbolic act against the temple. His teaching on
law observance was not such as to incline anyone to eliminate him from the scene, whether it
be "setting his own authority against that of
commandments of the Law" or "forgiving sins
in his own name." None of these stands up well
to scrutiny. Jesus could not have been found
blasphemous for any utterance attributed to
him before the first-century church theologized
his sayings. It is equally apparent, however,
that he was vulnerable in predicting the dissolution of the present condition of Jewish existence as the new and final age came on.

The Earliest Recall of Jesus' Sayings

Important in any hypothesis on the meaning of
Jesus' death is the impact his teaching about
God's impending rule would have had on his
disciples. The Gospels testify to the disciples'
incomprehension of Jesus' teaching. They
would surely have pondered after his resurrection, however, what his proclamation of the
final age meant for them. He had hinted at a
role for them in God's mysterious future. The

memory of Jesus' vision for the future would
have stayed with them. It would have accounted for their remaining together as a company, thinking of themselves as "the Twelve,"
as the assembly of the new age. In a word, the
continuity between Jesus' life and teaching in
an eschatological mode and the origins of a
community of believers in a similar mode reflects the compulsion they felt to conduct
themselves as if God's reign were already inau-
gurated. Without this as the main theme of
Jesus' teaching, the post-Easter activity of his
companions would be inexplicable.

The four evangelists and Paul all held fast to
a core of tradition that required Jesus' post-
Easter disciples to proclaim a reign of God that
was to come in its fullness, with Jesus as the
anointed human king already in heaven exer-
cising by anticipation the divine rule. Paul's vision of the way it would be consummated at the
end of the age spells out the Christ version of
this Jewish hope (1 Cor. 15:20-28).

With the memory of Jesus' insistence on the
sovereign kingship of God ringing in their ears
("May your kingdom come," Luke 11:2), the disciples did nothing strange or unpredictable in
designating Jesus king-messiah from the start.
He almost certainly never entertained the title
as describing himself, because its meaning as
successful liberator of Israel was fixed in the
popular mind. It had no biblical or postbiblical
history as a "spiritualized" title. Nothing in the

Gospel tradition indicates that Jesus wished to refashion its connotations away from the received political-religious one. The earliest post-resurrection disciples must simply have thought it right as a description of the risen one. He ended as a crucified Messiah because the reign of God he proclaimed was resisted by the rich and powerful. The title as applied to him would have brought on immediate ribald laughter. It was totally oxymoronic. This was a leader with whom no one had remained loyally except for a band of women and one man: a sorry end for one more failed messiah.

What made it enter anyone's mind initially to connect the name of Jesus with a term connoting royalty? His origins as a Bethlehemite by birth and his legal sonship from Joseph, a descendant of David, would have been known to his close friends (see Matt. 1:16; Luke 3:23; John 1:45). Even if Bethlehem were not his actual birthplace but became such in popular memory *because* he was Davidic, that would only confirm, not place in doubt, his origin as a man of Judah. The remembrance of Jesus being mocked as a king could also have had something to do with the early claims of believers in him that he was the Messiah, although the historicity of this narrative cannot be verified (see Mark 15:18; Matt. 27:29; John 19:3). The *titlos* on the cross denoting obliquely the charge against him may conceivably have been at the root of it: "King of Judea" (Mark 15:26; Matt.

27:37; Luke 23:38; John 19:19). Note well, that derisive placard seemed to say, the end of all such would-be usurpers. For believers in Jesus' resurrection the whitewashed board on the stake above his head would have in retrospect said something quite different: "This is the man who proclaimed a kingship of God" that began to be realized with his rising from the dead. The taunt of the one who sentenced him to death was prophetic: "Jesus of Nazareth, the king of the Jews [or of Judea]" (John 19:3, 14). This most improbable Messiah had begun to reign.

To call Jesus "messiah" (Greek, *christos*) at first blush looks like conscious paradox, a seizing on the least probable designation of him. Jesus' brief life as a public figure and his sorry end so completely contradicted the popular image of messiah that it is doubtful his disciples would have settled on such a rash verbal tour de force. Rather than furthering their cause it would only have invited mockery had they not solid reasons to employ it. They needed a better reason than a paradox intended to pique popular curiosity. Fidelity to their master's proclamation of God's coming kingdom and their conviction of his centrality in that reign would have been that reason. It was as the person anointed by God to preach God's reign that he was best remembered (see Luke 4:18, quoting Isa. 61:1-2). But, Jesus, the risen one, was identical with the crucified proclaimer of God's reign. Therefore he was remembered as Jesus

Messiah from an early date after his resurrection, giving that title a different meaning than the one it had traditionally had. He was a Jewish king in a quite new sense.

"The Christ"—But a Crucified One?

To call Jesus the Christ of God was to make a faith statement about his role in the future kingdom. It said nothing about his death on the cross as atoning for sins. In fact, it did quite the opposite. The concepts "messiah" and "suffering" are nowhere coupled in contemporary Jewish writings, diligently as Christian theologians have searched for the conjunction. In some postbiblical visions of the end, God's Messiah would act as judge of humankind. Nowhere, however, was this central figure of judgment, by whatever title, seen as suffering—let alone dying. Far from dying in the final encounter with evil, he was to be the victor in the name of all the living.

Obviously, then, Jesus' undergoing an atoning death as the Christ cannot derive from any existing model. Could the explanation be simpler? He had died in shameful circumstances and there was no getting around the fact. Therefore, the earliest believers might have reasoned, why not make the best of it? A noble or sublime interpretation of the harsh realities of his execution might neutralize the sting of his death. Sentences of proclamation found positive virtue in his death, such as an early one, he "died for our sins in accordance with the scriptures" (1 Cor. 15:3). The death was presented as expiatory from the first we hear of it, which was probably in the pre-Pauline fragment quoted in Romans 3:25-26; but more of that below.

Do We Have Jesus' View of Why He Died?

One way to account for this early belief that Jesus "died for our sins" might be that Jesus himself viewed his impending death as expiatory by God's design. If this could be proved, the search need go no further than his own words on the subject. The difficulty is that we do not have them. The two places in the earliest Gospel, Mark, where Jesus speaks of the meaning of his death cannot be shown to be original with him. Putting them under scrutiny (the texts are Mark 10:45 and 14:24) reveals them to be interpretations put on his death in later, probably Greek-speaking circles.

The context of the first is that the true greatness of a disciple consists in service rather than arrogance or dominion (10:42-44). The saying that comes next, v. 45a, seems to have originated in a different context, namely, a polemic against the idea that the eschatological Son of man was to be served when he came. Aside from the probability that the title "Son of man"

as attributed to Jesus was the work of the early
church, giving his life "as a ransom for the
many" (v. 45b) may have derived from the early
faith conviction that he had indeed "fulfilled"
the prophecy of Isaiah 53: "Through his suffering, my servant shall justify many. . . . He shall
take away the sins of many, and win pardon for
their offenses" (Isa. 53:11, 12). The one Gospel
citation of that fourth Servant Song (Isa.
52:13–53:12) relates it to Jesus' cures of the
sick, not to his self-perception (see Matt. 8:17).
Besides, it is a case of Matthew's view of Jesus,
not Jesus' view of himself. In the form in which
the Mark quotation appears, "The Son of man
. . . [came] to give his life as a ransom for the
many" (10:45) is the conviction of the Markan
church that Jesus was a vicarious sufferer on
humanity's behalf.[3]

The saying of Jesus over the cup at the last
meal he ate with his friends labors under the
same difficulties: "This is my blood of the
covenant which is poured out for many" (Mark
14:24). Matthew retains the entire phrase,
adding "for the forgiveness of sins" (26:28),
while Luke has "shed for you" (22:20). Paul
names as the effect of drinking from this cup in
faith a sealing of "the new covenant in my
blood," calling it a proclamation of the LORD's
death until he come (1 Cor. 11:25b-26). The four
versions of Jesus' words over the bread and
wine at the supper table were evidently four
liturgical formulas that developed in four local

churches. We cannot be sure of Jesus' precise words on which they were based. Mark's "which is poured out for many" of 14:24 clearly accords with his theology of Jesus' vicarious death found in 10:45. It may well either underlie (in Matthew) or be common to (in Luke and Paul) the development of thought in other churches. Attributing an expiatory purpose to Jesus' death by his own expressed intent does not, in any case, seem to be grounded in any Gospel text. Broadening this statement, no word of Jesus that can be maintained as authentically his indicates what his state of mind was as to the effect of his death.

The Maccabean Martyrs as Paradigm of Jesus' Death

We find reference to the deaths of the martyrs of the Maccabean period (167–75 B.C.E.) in the following places: Daniel 11:32-35; 12:1-3; *Testament* (or *Assumption*) *of Moses* 8; 9; 1 Maccabees 1–5; Josephus, *Antiquities* 12.241–13.214 (which is a paraphrase of 1 Macc. 1:14–13:42); and 2 Maccabees 5:12-14, 24-26; 6; 7. Could the view of the deaths of the righteous Israelites in these writings have influenced the earliest Christian interpretation of the death of Jesus?

Daniel may contain the earliest references to the fate of those Jews who died in the persecution of Antiochus Epiphanes around 165. A despicable person "who shall seize the kingdom by stealth and fraud" (Dan. 11:21) will cause some who are disloyal to the covenant to apostatize (v. 32) and punish with the sword, exile, plunder, and flames the nation's wise, who shall instruct the many (v. 33). Few people shall assist the wise as they fall victim (the aggressive Maccabees?) and many shall join them out of insincere motives (v. 34).

The book of Daniel had previously alluded to the suffering and death of those Jews who held fast to the Law ("the holy ones") and could not be forced into apostasy by the tyrant (see 7:21, 25; 8:24, 25). Nowhere, however, is there mention of the effect of the deaths of the faithful on others. We are left to conclude from what is not said that the death of some of the teachers has purified others by putting them to the test. The time is "unsurpassed in distress" (12:1), but the warriors and others who are slaughtered shall rise from the dust, the innocent to the life of the final age but some to everlasting disgrace (v. 2). There is a reward in prospect for the wise and those who lead many to justice. They shall be "resplendent like the firmament . . . be like the stars forever" (12:3). But for those who die in fidelity to the covenant the reward of resurrection is personal. Their deaths will achieve a boon for themselves but nothing for others.

First Maccabees, written about 100 B.C.E. concerning the events from 167–65 B.C.E. down to 134, is not notably different in theme from

Daniel, except that the author of 1 Maccabees
does not hold out to the just who die for the law
the personal reward of being raised up from the
grave. Heroic deaths in testimony to the law
will result in an everlasting name for those who
die, but we are left to conclude that their sole
legacy to the living will be their courageous
example (see 1 Macc. 2:50, 51, 61, 74).

Second Maccabees sees the Maccabean persecution "in terms of man's sin and God's
wrath," without "making the connection between the martyrs' deaths and Israel's deliverance.[4] Those who die will receive, after brief
pain, a life that never fails (7:36). The book, in
sum, does not suggest any direct cause-effect
relation between the deaths of the martyrs and
the deliverance of Israel.

In all this one should note that nowhere in
the New Testament was Jesus remembered to
have died at Gentile hands for fidelity to the
law or the deliverance of Israel from Gentile
oppression. Nonetheless, the question remains,
Could the memory of the deaths of the martyrs
have influenced the earliest proclamation of
him as a messiah who atoned for sins by his
death? Some say that the notion of his death as
expiatory could not have flourished in the earliest church were it not for the Jewish cult of
the martyrs. One cannot, of course, prove that
such was *not* the case. The question is whether
evidence can be summoned to establish that it
was the case. The replication of the Seleucid

dynasty's cruelty two centuries before was surely etched in the mind of every Jew who believed in Jesus. Still, the search for specific common elements between Jesus' death and that of the martyred thousands yields very few. Both he and they died for their loyalty to the God of Israel, but they for ritual purity and covenant fidelity, he (in the interpretation of early believers) for enunciating the terms of a reign of God to come. His first disciples found in his death the supreme benefit of the rectification of a humanitywide ill. The more important question is, Is there anything like this vicarious sacrifice in the Bible? It can be either one person dying for others or any sacrificial act that is widely believed to profit the many. If such a sacrifice is present, even in a general way, we need only say that the paradigm existed ready-made.

The Bible and Expiation by the Deaths of Others

Throughout most of the biblical period death is viewed as God's punishment for sin. Suffering is likewise seen as retributive. From the earliest biblical books down through the writings attributed to the Deuteronomist and the Chronicler, some act of wrongdoing is sought to account for every misfortune. The dawning of a new outlook on the causes of suffering came after the exile. With an increased appreciation of the

worth and responsibility of individuals came
less satisfaction with the idea of future reward
for the community as an adequate explanation
of individual suffering. The author of Job wres-
tled with the problem mightily but concluded
that the mystery was beyond him. He found his
solution in the inexplicable majesty of God. The
most usual explanation of suffering in this period of Judaism was that God permitted it to test
persons in their misfortune. We find this in the
first two chapters of Job, where God permits
Satan to submit this man of Uz to many trials to
see if he will curse God.

Deaths in the Bible and immediately after are
a personal misfortune in the many cases where
they have no retributive character, but no positive value is assigned to them. Warriors die because it is the will of God; they may derive
some benefit for Israel out of their victory. They
do not give their lives out of patriotic self-sac-
rifice as in the familiar Greek model. Sometimes
individuals in the Bible die to appease YHWH's
wrath or to rid the people of transgressors of
the covenant, but they never die with the *purpose* of achieving a good.

Do any Hebrew Scriptures claim that one
person's suffering or dying achieves expiation
for the sins of others? Moses seems to make
such an offer to the LORD for the people's sin of
casting the molten calf, but it is not clear if his
proposal is one of sacrificial mediation. Besides,
"strike me out of the book you have written" is

in itself an ambiguous phrase (Exod. 32:32). If could mean simply "forget me." The LORD's response settles the question; Moses' offer is not allowed: "Him only who has sinned against me will I strike out of my book" (v. 33). Personal responsibility is at issue here.

In the scapegoat passage that underlies the Day of Atonement, the community's sins are transferred symbolically to a single beast (see Lev. 16:15-22) by "confessing over it all the sinful faults and transgressions of the Israelites" (v. 21). The animal in this rite is accepted by God as a pleasing sacrifice. God then removes the people's sins *if* the symbolic victim conveys their repentant state of heart. It cannot be established that this or any sacrifice of birds or beasts accomplished a transfer such that their deaths were thought accepted by God in place of the deaths of humans who should be dying for their own sins. The transgressions atoned for were normally not deserving of death, and an expiation that did not engage the human will was as abhorrent to the Israelite as it would be later to the Christian.

This brings us to the one passage in Israel's Scriptures that is widely supposed by Christian theologians to lie behind the Gospel narratives of the passion even though no evangelist employs it there, namely, Isaiah 52:13–53:12. (Matthew 27:30 is a remote echo of Isa. 50:6, while Luke 22:37, "And he was reckoned among the transgressors," Isa. 53:12c, does little other than declare Jesus' innocence. Luke does quote the passage at Acts 8:32.) It is the prime candidate for what was intended by the words "died for our since according to the Scriptures" in 1 Corinthians 15:3. The question is, What does "he was wounded for our transgressions, crushed for our iniquities" (Isa. 53:5a) mean? Is this a true case of vicarious, expiatory suffering? Or did a faithful servant of God simply have to endure the punishment that was meted out to a wicked people? "Upon him was the punishment that made us whole, and by his bruises we are healed"—but in what sense? Is it mere hyperbole?

Everything hinges on what is meant by the "healing" and "making whole" of 53:5b, the "being smitten for the sin of his people" (v. 8). The guilt of us all was laid on him (v. 6). Was he simply made the paradigm of the people's guilt without further effect, a symbol of its wrongdoing in which he had no part? Or did God accept the chastisement he bore to remove the guilt incurred? In the latter case, what the servant suffered is being described as advantageous to many. Israel has sinned and been carried off into exile as a result of its sin. The servant's acceptance of suffering, it seems, has something to do with rectifying the situation by removing what God has against this people. If an individual is not being spoken of and Israel is itself the servant, then Second Isaiah may be describing the people's being brought low in humble acquiescence at the means God intends to bring about a change in its fortunes.

If Isaiah 53 had had any influence on the thinking of Palestinian believers in Jesus, we might expect it to have surfaced somewhere in the four passion narratives. Their sources, after all, were Palestinian in origin. Yet no such use of either passage occurs, despite the fact that Matthew revels in such quotations when they seem apt. John employs biblical allusions rather than direct citations. Yet neither he nor Matthew employs it. The roots of the early doctrine of Jesus' death as saving do not, therefore, seem to lie in the Suffering Servant of Isaiah or in any other pre-Christian text. Neither Paul nor any evangelist saw fit to find in this passage the paradigm for Jesus' expiatory death.

The Inspiration of Paul's Soteriology

Some passages in 4 Maccabees, dated between 18 and 55 C.E., seem unique for the time leading up to or just after Jesus' death. One of these that is claimed to have influenced the way Paul viewed Jesus' death as salvific is as follows:

> [Through the martyrs] the tyrant was punished and our land purified, since they became, as it were, a ransom for the sin of our nation. Through the blood of these righteous ones and through the propitiation of their death the divine providence rescued Israel, which had been shamefully treated. (17:21-22)

The language of ransom, purification, and
expiation derives in its entirety from the Greek
translation of the Jewish Scriptures (the Septuagint). The author in speaking of "the sin of our
nation" (17:21) means widespread apostasy.
Whether the sins be weighty or light, they all
equally set the law at nought (see 5:19-21). The
main intent of the treatise, however, is to incul-
cate the "mastery of the passions by devout reason" (1:1), specifically as exemplified by the
endurance of the nine martyrs under torture on
whom it concentrates. The vocabulary of this
concept occurs throughout. The example the
martyrs give to others of adhering to the law
(7:9), thereby living the life of the age of blessing (17:18; cf. 18:23), makes them "responsible
for the downfall of the tyranny that beset our
nation . . . so that through them their own land
was purified" (1:11). This quite objective result is
attributed to the sufferings and deaths of the resisters. In light of their self-offering the LORD restored to Israel its land, "as it were a ransom for
the sin of our nation" (17:21). God accepted the
offering of their lives as an expiatory sacrifice.

Jews did not preserve 4 Maccabees; Christians did. Second-century and later Christian
writers made use of it. But can it be shown to
have had currency in Hellenistic Jewish circles
that could have influenced New Testament
thinking directly? The one place in Paul's writings that reflects it most faithfully has been referred to above, Romans 3:25-26.

Some think that a primitive formulation lies behind Romans 3 and had as its purpose to explain how God, out of restraint, has not punished the sins of the Gentiles up to now but has taken positive action in Christ to deal with them. Paul writes that "all [i.e., Jews and non-Jews alike] are justified freely by God's grace through the redemption of Christ Jesus" (v. 24). This is followed by the verses that are presumed to be the citation of a pre-Pauline source:

> For God designed him to be the means of expiating [*hilastērion*] sin by his blood, effective through faith. God meant by this to demonstrate [the divine] justice, because out of forbearance God had overlooked the sins of the past—to demonstrate this justice now in the present, showing that God is himself just and justifies anyone who has faith in Jesus. (Rom. 3:25-26)

Hilastērion here has to be expiatory, because "past sins" is the subject of "passing over" and "forbearance." The passage of 4 Maccabees that is thought to underlie the Pauline source reads: "Through the blood of these pious ones and through the expiation [*hilastērion*] of their death the divine providence rescued Israel" (17:22). There is no closer parallel in all pre-Pauline Jewish literature to the shedding of Christ's blood as expiatory—as achieving a benefit for Jews and Gentiles alike—than the passage just cited. Eleazar had petitioned: "Be merciful to your people and let our punishment be a satisfaction on their behalf. Make my blood their purification and take my life as a ransom for theirs" (4 Macc. 6:29). The words that are common to the two texts of 4 Maccabees, "purification," "ransom," and "expiatory" (*katharsion, antipsychon, hilastērios*) are not found in Greek versions of the Bible except for *hilastērios,* which in Exodus 25:17 describes the lid of the ark. The roots of the other two words frequently refer to purification and expiation. Proponents of the thesis regret that they cannot prove that Antioch was the place where 4 Maccabees was written, thinking it would establish that Paul first heard the idea of Christ's death as expiatory developed there.[5] It is at least demonstrable that tales of the Maccabean martyrs were developing in Greek-speaking Judaism in a way that made it impossible for the first believers in Jesus—even among Palestinian Jews—not to be familiar with them.

Tracking Paul's Usage Further

A few other passages in Paul's correspondence have been suggested as containing his inheritance from earlier Christians in this matter. Two of them are remnants of pre-Pauline material, Galatians 4:4-8 (v. 5 parallels 3:13 in verb use) and Romans 8:31-34.[6] A third, Gala-

tians 3:13, is Paul's original development. In
the first passage God sends forth the Son in
order to buy freedom (v. 5) for the Jews, just as
God has sent forth the Spirit of the Son to turn
Gentile slaves into children of God (vv. 6-8). As
regards the Jews, there is no mention of how
the Son redeems them. But Paul's verb *exapos-
tellō* (send forth) used in Galatians 4:4 and 6
occurs nowhere else in his letters. In the two
biblical cases where one redeems or buys freedom for another, a priest "sends out" a live bird
once he has symbolically transferred the impu-
rity of leprosy to it (Lev. 14:7) and "sends
out" a goat into the desert once he has made
the symbolic transfer to it of the people's sins
(Lev. 16:10).

Galatians 3:13 similarly has the language of
redemption. Paul says there that Jesus' death
"bought us [Jews] freedom from the curse of the
law," namely, that incurred by not "doing
everything that is written in the book of the
law" (v. 10), by "coming under the curse [of cru-
cifixion] for our sake" (3:13). He probably
means by his language that Jesus' death accomplished what would set Israel perfectly
right in God's eyes, which, as we learn from
elsewhere in his letters, he did not think the law
could do. If the "sending out" that Paul is most
familiar with has a redemptive connotation
(and the scapegoat certainly died in achieving
its redemptive purpose), an explanation would
be ready to hand for how Jesus' death operated

on human behalf. His life would have been thought of as accepted by God for the sins of the people as an accursed one (Deut. 21:23) redeeming others under a curse. Noteworthy is the fact that several early Christian texts (for example, *Barnabas* 7.6-11; Justin, *Dialogue with Trypho* 40.4; and Tertullian, *Against Marcion* 3.7.7) employ the scapegoat figure to illustrate Christ's death.

As to the influence of the stories of the Maccabean martyrs on a primitive conviction that Jesus' death was expiatory, it is easy to say, if not "with certainty," that at the time of his crucifixion "the notion of vicarious suffering and passive response to persecution were firmly embedded in Judean consciousness."[7] That generalized fact does not seem sufficient to account for the primitive doctrine that Jesus' death was expiatory for the whole human race. He simply was never considered by those who believed in him to be one Jewish martyr among the many who had died at gentile hands.

On balance, it appears that none of the above images of human sacrifice was responsible for the pre-Pauline conviction of Christians that Jesus had died to expiate sins. Only the Jewish conviction of the efficacy of temple sacrifice in its totality, it seems, could do this. An integral part of this expiatory belief was the conviction that his body was the new temple—glorious now but once offered on the altar of the cross.

How the Cross Came to Be Seen as Redemptive

Paul is the earliest witness we have to belief in Jesus' death on Calvary as expiating human sin and sinfulness. His correspondence from the 50s does not illumine us directly on how this death was viewed in its effects in Jewish Palestine in the 30s and 40s. It does serve, however, as an important cross-reference to the Palestinian traditions on the matter that survived to be included in the Gospels. What is astonishing is that Paul "appears totally uninterested in tracking down and identifying the villains responsible for Jesus' crucifixion, nor does he offer any historical reasons why they did it."[8] The possible exception of 1 Thessalonians 2:14-15 has been noted above. Paul interprets Jesus' death apocalyptically rather than historically in statements such as, "None of the rulers of this age understood this [i.e., the secret wisdom of God decreed before the ages]; for if they had, they would not have crucified the LORD of glory" (1 Cor. 2:8). These rulers, to judge from the context, are not Caiaphas or Pilate but the cosmic forces of the present evil age that are destined to pass away (see v. 6). Paul's overriding interest is not in evil men who have done a wicked thing but in a good God who has done a gracious thing. (On this, see Rom. 5:8, where God is the protagonist behind Jesus' death, and Gal. 1:4, where Jesus takes the initiative but in compliance with God's will.) At all points Paul sees the mystery of Calvary in terms of God's action. In 1 Corinthians 1:18–2:5, for example, the cross is viewed as an expression of the divine wisdom. God is self-revealed as a saving God in the preaching of the cross.

Whether Romans 3:25-26 is a pre-Pauline formula of Christian Jews, or Paul's own synagogue composition on the Day of Atonement, or a post-Pauline interpolation in the middle of a Pauline sentence, it is a clear statement of God's being just in overlooking previously committed sins and the designation of Christ Jesus as "the means of expiating (*hilastērion*) sin by his death."[9] Before it is anything else, Christ's death is proof of God's love for us (Rom. 5:6-8). Nowhere in Paul does one find the notion of a suffering or crucified God, certainly not in the statement that Christ was delivered up for us all (Rom. 8:32). The furthest we can go in the direction of God as fellow sufferer is to cite Romans 8:5: "God shows his own love for us in that Christ died for us while we were still sinners." Loving, yes, but suffering as Jesus did in dying for us—not that.

Many texts in Paul's letters mention Jesus' death in terms of human sinfulness. That he "gave himself for our sins" is stated in Galatians 1:4, with repetitions or echoes in Romans 5:6, 8; 14:15; 1 Thessalonians 5:10; 2 Corinthians 5:14; Galatians 2:20; 3:13. The question has often been raised whether there was such a widespread consciousness of sin among first-century Jews that Jesus' followers would immediately have identified his death and resurrection with a divine response to the human predicament of alienation from God. Conformity to God's will was, after all, humanity's true goal for Israel, so failure to meet it should have ranked high as a test of Jewish fidelity.

The whole rhythm of temple sacrifice was geared to restore worshipers who had disturbed a right relation with God by conscious or unconscious sin to a balance of forgiveness. A careful examination of biblical and postbiblical writing should convince anyone that a consciousness of personal and corporate sin was at the heart of Israel's religion. The whole of temple sacrifice was geared to liberating the people from the effects of sin.

For that reason it should not surprise us that, when an innocent man was viewed as yielding up his life freely, he should have been seen as an offering for sin. That Israel repudiated human sacrifice should not have posed a barrier. The whole Jewish culture was familiar with animal victims symbolic of the repentant human spirit. It was a short step from there to seeing in this sinless human victim Jesus an expiatory sin offering.

Paul reminded the former pagans of Thessalonica that they were waiting for the risen Son of God, now in heaven, to come and begin the process of judgment, this "Jesus who delivers us from the approaching wrath" (1 Thess. 1:9b-10). Gentile proselytes to Judaism were probably familiar with a similar promise about relief from the divine judgment if they would associate themselves with God's people. Paul sees faith in the crucified and risen one as the fulfillment of end-time promise. See 4;13-14 and 5:9-10 for other statements of the same hope. In the latter, his death is "for (*hyper*) us," enlarged in 2 Corinthians 5:14-15 to "he has died for all." The former pagan is "the fellow believer for whom Christ died" (1 Cor. 8:11).

Eating the flesh and drinking the blood of enemies is a repulsive figure in the Bible (see Isa. 49:26; Ezek. 39:17-20), but the early believers in Jesus gave it new mythic significance as they made such eating and drinking an image of solidarity with the victim of the cross (1 Cor. 10:16; see the parallels in the Last Supper wording of Mark 14:22-24; Matt. 26:26-27; Luke 22:17-19; 1 Cor. 11:24-26; cf. John 6:54-56). The blood of temple sacrifice was smeared, then flung on the stones of the altar by the priests who had title to the choicest portions of the animals' flesh (see Lev. 9:8-14; 10:12-15). Ordinary worshipers also ate of the victims offered in proof of solidarity in repentant victimhood, for these beasts represented the contrite hearts of a sinful people.

It is thus no wonder that the blood of the innocent Jesus began to be thought of as resealing the ancient covenant between God and

Israel (1 Cor. 11:25; Luke 22:20), this time a new covenant in prophetic fulfillment (see Jer. 31:31) of being final in its effect. When the various early communities partook of this ritual meal they experienced Jesus present in their midst, his body crucified and his blood shed but now in glory, as their spiritual food and drink. They were one with the victim who had been provided them by a gracious God to reconcile them to God and to each other.

The Gospel of John makes Caiaphas remark at 11:50: "It is expedient for you that one man should die for the people." This can be taken as either the callous comment of one who favors sacrificing an individual for the greater good or, in a supreme expression of irony, as unconscious affirmation of Jesus' death as a boon to Israel. That the deaths of the martyrs were on people's minds as "having become as it were, a ransom (*antipsychon*) for our nation's sins" (4 Macc. 17:22) has already been shown as a possibility, but the setting of such an idea "seems to belong to a period of major conflict not evident in the formal expression of 'He died—he rose' and so may be put aside."[10] The traditional formula that speaks of Jesus' death and resurrection "for our sins," 1 Corinthians 15:1-7, was one that Paul said he received and handed on. His insistence in his letter to the Galatians (1:18, 23) that he had spent two weeks with Peter (Cephas) three years after becoming a believer should provide some assurance that the "good news of faith" he set about proclaiming already had this reconciling death and resurrection at its core.

In identifying temple sacrifice as the paradigm for the earliest conviction that Jesus' death had a beneficent effect on Israel, and with it all humanity, I am not disregarding the passages in the biblical and postbiblical books reviewed above that seem to speak of a vicarious sacrifice by human victims. It is only that they appear to have been resorted to after decades of reflection, whereas the parallel between the shedding of the blood of innocent beasts in expiation of sins and that of the innocent Jesus was staring the first disciples in the face. How could recourse to various places in the sacred books account for something much better accounted for by the great, daily act of Israel's living religion? A "people of the Book" the learned among the postexilic Jews certainly were, but for the great bulk of them circumcision, the Sabbath, the food laws, and temple sacrifice *were* the religious tradition. The sacrifices went on quite uninterrupted by Jesus' death and resurrection. Acts could describe the daily temple ritual decades later as something his disciples resumed as a matter of course (2:46). But their reflection on the turning over of the just one to a pagan court by the very guardians of temple worship must have made a profound impression.

The high priest and his associates were a corrupt lot, but that distressing fact was long known to the populace. Could the impenetrable mystery of Jesus' uprising from the dead be best explained as God's revelation of the meaning of his death? They had always called him the Teacher. Might he not also be God's Anointed in a transcendent sense—more than that, the focal point of a pure worship of God in a new age? In that age the temple and its ritual would have no place. A people that had no need of expiation for sin was unthinkable, especially for this latest sin. The step to seeing in Jesus the victim of a perfect sacrifice was a short one. A recurrent memorial rather than a once-yearly meal to make the effects of this sacrifice available would have been an early step. We do not know the steps because they are not recorded, but that it so happened we cannot easily doubt. Within two decades this way of looking at Jesus' death and resurrection and the final meal that preceded it was firmly in place.

The way chosen was the way of myth, just as Israel's deliverance from Egypt and the return from exile and the slaughter by the Seleucids were commemorated mythically. The events were remembered history but they were not remembered *as* history. To be sure, fragments of the actual happenings were retained. Even so, these are mythicized as they appear in the Gospels and Acts. The stress is not on the cross and its horrors but on the death. It was coerced, like all such judicial executions, but in the myth it was seen as voluntary. Jesus' thoughts on his being led to death are not known. It was interpreted as a deed of God, perhaps based on what underlay his statements in the Gospels that by God's will it had to happen so. In any case, the death of Jesus survived in the church's weekly ritual commemoration as the painful preliminary to his exaltation. The two together constituted a human although God-authored atonement for human sin. The apocalyptic view of avoidance of the divine wrath is present—a concept a world away from placating an angry god by a savage letting of blood. No such conception as that appears in the earliest records we have.

There stands apart only a death which, from the first, is given a faith interpretation. Concentration on that death as the sum of its historical details comes much later. It is the product of a demonic mythologizing that popular religion is so good at and true religion so ineffective in exorcising.

3

How Jesus' Death Was Blamed on "the Jews"

The twenty-seven books that became the New Testament canon were written in Greek in various unknown places in the Jewish diaspora. Only a letter or two of Paul's can be traced to its probable place of origin. These are Hellenized Jewish writings, some of them fairly remote from Palestinian life. All, however, are concerned to maintain links with Israel, the religion of the writers. Indeed, they think that belief in Jesus Christ and the Spirit common to him and the Father is the true way for Jews and non-Jews alike to profess the religion of Israel.

As pointed out in chapter 1, the writings of the New Testament had an apologetic cast. Subtle and at times overt appeals were made, not to pagans generally or even to the officials of the empire for favored treatment such as

Jews received (these would come much later), but to Greek-speaking Jews. It was they whom believers in Jesus hoped to influence. But, as with the Hebrew Scriptures, the Christian writings contain charges against some Jews in power for infidelity to the covenant as the writers perceived it. This was not a simple diaspora-Judea struggle but one narrowed down to two groups: the learned among the evangelists' contemporaries (who become "the scribes and Pharisees") and the remembered temple priesthood (called "the chief priests") who were coupled with "the elders" when the Sanhedrin was meant (in John, "the men of Judea").

Jewish disciples of the risen Christ, like believers in him of later ages, could not comprehend how their fellow religionists could fail to be convinced by their arguments. To these arguments they added charges of resistance to the truth by their forebears. It is as wrong to call this polemic in the New Testament "anti-Semitism" as it would be to speak of anti-Semitism in the books of the prophets or the Dead Sea Scrolls. The New Testament thrusts were one side of the internal polemic of Jews (with some ethnic non-Jews on that side) that provided the raw material for anti-Judaism on the part of a Gentile church in the next century. When this contending faction became largely Gentile, religious or theological anti-Judaism was the correct name for the phenomenon. The Jewish anti-Christianism of the same period has left only faint traces in the Mishnah and its commentary, the Gemara, but one can assume it was equally vigorous. Such was the religious spirit of the times. There was no other way for religions, including the various paganisms, to go.

Justin

The effect was not immediate, however. Of the second-century witnesses whose writings we have, only Justin in mid-century and Melito of Sardis toward the end seem to take it for granted that "the Jews" should be identified with Jesus' death. The *Didachē*, Ignatius, *1 Clement*, *Barnabas*, the *Epistle of Polycarp*, and the *Martyrdom of Polycarp* refer to Jesus' death, but without giving it an anti-Jewish interpretation.

Justin was a pagan native of Shechem in Samaria, modern Nablus (Flavia Neapolis). He couples Samaritans with Jews as possessing the books of prophecy, the Torah, as no Jew would do (53). We do not know the circumstances of his becoming a Christian aside from his expressed admiration for the Christian martyrs.[1] He was put to death for his faith at Rome,[2] but we do not know the circumstances of his journeyings. Thus we cannot determine where he experienced the mutual hatred between Christians and Jews ("slanders uttered against those who confess Christ," *1 Apology* 49). He gave expression to it from the Christian side in describing the indignities visited on Jesus in his passion, chiefly from passages in Isaiah and the Psalms; but he was also familiar with the mockery of passersby, chief priests, and scribes reported in Mark 15:29-32. Justin concludes this account with: "And that all these things happened to Christ at the hand of the Jews, you can ascertain" (38).

Justin's first *Apology* (ca. 155) defends the Christian faith for its reasonableness, holding that the pagans accept far more that is incredible in their myths than the Christians do in their mysteries. He writes that Jesus Christ was born for the purpose of teaching us the things that would lead to our living again in incorruption, and immediately goes on to say: "and was crucified under Pontius Pilate who was procurator of Judea in the time of Tiberius Caesar" (13; cf. 46; *2 Apology* 6). The Jews had their own ruler and king, Justin observes, up to the time when Jesus Christ came to fulfill the unrecognized prophecies in a book of Moses like the one to Judah, one of Jacob's twelve sons in Genesis 49:10-11 (32). He identifies Herod Antipas as the Jews' king and conspirator with Pilate against Christ (40). Jesus "was crucified in Judea," Justin writes, "immediately after which the land of the Jews fell to you [Romans] as a spoil of war" (32; cf. 53). He points to no cause and effect here, as later writers will do.

Using the prophecies of Isaiah 11:1 and 51:15, Numbers 24:17 (32), and Isaiah 7:14, he traces Jesus' ancestry from Judah through

David ("the root of Jesse") to the virgin who bore him (33). Then, coming to the final days of Jesus Christ, Justin writes: He "stretched out his hands when he was crucified by the Jews, who contradicted him and denied that he was the Christ" (35). Justin's sources for the passion narrative are obscure here. The quotation from Zechariah 9:9 in Matthew 21:5 is attributed to Zephaniah. Jesus' being mocked by the soldiers is made out to be a quotation from a prophet, but it occurs in a form that is unattested. Justin refers to the *Acts of Pilate,* an apocryphal Christian document that contains much of this material (48).[3] In any case, Justin has the following charge embedded in an otherwise perceptive paragraph about the various genres of biblical writing: "Not understanding [them], the Jews who are in possession of the books of the prophets did not recognize Christ even when he came, and they hate us who declare that he has come and show that he was crucified by them as had been predicted" (36; cf. 49, where this charge is repeated).

When Justin comes to write his *Dialogue with Trypho*—well after his *1 Apology* (see chap. 80) but as if the exchange occurred shortly after the Bar Kokhba revolt in 135 (chap. 1)—he goes on the assumption that Jews are at fault in not reading biblical "prophecies" as referring to Jesus, as he and other Christians do. For him, "a later covenant voids an older one" (11). This is the earliest expression we have, after Hebrews

8:7, 13, of belief in the supersession or replacement of Judaism by Christianity. (But see Eph. 2:15, which states "[Christ] abolished the law," a verb Paul would not have used. "Law" here seems to mean the ritual precepts no longer required for Gentiles.) Justin thinks that ritual observance in its entirety, including circumcision, keeping the Sabbath, and fasting, has yielded to abstention from perjury, theft, adultery (12), anger, avarice, jealousy, and hatred (14). The whole body of ritual precepts was imposed on the Jews because of their sins and hardness of heart (18). Circumcision was given to Israel with God's foreknowledge that it would serve as a sign to the Romans to keep Jews from entering Jerusalem, the capital of their "desolate land with its cities ruined by fire" (16; cf. 19). This judgment on Jews over Hadrian's sack of Jerusalem is unspeakably harsh. Justin thinks it justified because he has evidently heard that "you dishonor and curse in your synagogues all who believe in Christ [although] now you cannot use violence against us Christians because of those who are in power [the later years of the peaceful reign of Antoninus Pius?], but as often as you could, you did employ force against us" (16; cf. 96).

Whatever harassments Justin has in mind, whether reality or rumor, he is able to write that "the other nations have not treated Christ and us, his followers, as unjustly as have you Jews. . . . After you had crucified the only sinless and just man . . . you not only failed to feel remorse for your evil deed but you even dispatched certain picked men from Jerusalem to every land to report the godless heresy of the Christians" (17). This sounds like a reality of some kind within the Jewish community in Rome where Justin resides, which makes Christian proclaiming of the gospel as a legitimate understanding of the Jewish Scriptures hard or impossible. Whatever form Jewish opposition to the Christian movement took in the second century, this antipathy survived in the talmudic writings as a sprinkling of tales about a magician named Yeshu (the son of "Pantere" or "Pandera" in several second-century texts) who was hanged on the eve of Passover.[4] Most Christians could not read mishnaic Hebrew or Aramaic, and so these slanders seldom reached their ears, although the pagan Celsus knew of them in the third century.

The Christian opposition to Judaism, according to Justin, took the form of an accusation of responsibility for Jesus' crucifixion. The chief texts are: "He was pierced by you" (32); "was crucified and died after enduring suffering inflicted on him by your own people" (67); "the Jews planned to crucify Christ himself and to slay him" (72). When Pilate is mentioned he is simply used to date Jesus' death (76) or is someone before whom Jesus appeared (102). The undiluted accusations made by Justin against the Jews were picked up and repeated in the vernacular, Greek (then Latin, Syriac, and Coptic), everywhere there were Christians.

Justin's invariable coupling of the harassment of Christians by Jews with mention of Jewish responsibility for Jesus' death makes one wonder how much the former was a factor in interpreting the community reminiscences of the crucifixion that were incorporated in the Gospel accounts. In examining antipathies that go back five generations, as in this case, it is almost impossible to isolate the various factors. The repeated fueling of fires is a constant in such situations. It would seem that the mid-second-century accusations derive from more than recourse to the written New Testament tradition. A memory of subsequent experiences on both sides seems very much part of the story.

Justin seems to be making a genuine appeal when he asks Trypho's "brothers" not to "speak harshly against the Crucified . . . insult the Son of God . . . [or] scorn the King of Israel (as the chiefs of your synagogues instruct you to do after prayers)" (41). One can understand, of course, Jewish resistance to such exalted claims made for Jesus.

The origins of the treatise, dedicated as it is to a certain Marcus Pompeius, are puzzling. It seems to be a handbook designed to instruct the learned, whom Justin was arming in Rome against Jewish arguments that stressed the illegitimacy of the Christian movement. The likelihood that it reports actual, sustained Christian-

Jewish debate is small. Still, it is impossible to sort out what might have been its original, confrontational core aside from saying that it took its rise from exchanges with a peaceful rabbi.

Irenaeus and Melito

Irenaeus, writing in Lugdunum (Lyon) two decades later than Justin, possessed the bulk of the New Testament. This Greek-speaking Syrian went as a missionary bishop to Gaul after a stay in Rome, where he may have been Justin's pupil. While residing among the Celts with their "barbarous language," he did some careful research into the teachings of the Gnostics, whether recognizably Christian or other. This he reported in five books directed against them.[5] His chief concern was to unmask their myths as absurdities and to affirm the corporeal reality of Jesus' birth, career, death, and resurrection against the Gnostic denial that anything material can be of God. He does not reach the account of Jesus' career until book 3, chaps. 9–12. In laying out the preaching of the apostles like Peter and John reported in early Acts, Irenaeus speaks of their heavy task in presenting him "whom the Jews had seen as a man, and had fastened to the cross, . . . as Christ the Son of God, their eternal King. . . . They . . . told them to their face that they were the slayers of the Lord. . . . They . . . fastened to the cross the Savior superior to them (to whom it behooved them to ascend)."[6]

Irenaeus takes for granted Jewish responsibility for Jesus' death. Most of the quotations in section 7 are from Acts 10, for example: "the Jews [Judeans?] . . . put him to death by hanging him on a tree" (v. 39). He returns to the theme in his own words: "To the Jews [the apostles proclaimed] that the Jesus who was crucified by them was the Son of God, the judge of the living and the dead" (13). His suffering "under Pontius Pilate" likewise appears, a phrase we come to expect in these early writings (8). The emphasis is that Jesus really suffered for us, not some Christ incapable of suffering who descended on him (3.18.3; cf. 4.33.2).

One does not find as much animus toward the Jews in this lengthy treatise as in Justin. When it does surface, it is taken for granted as if it derives from catechetical formulas already arrived at. Thus, in a discussion of how God's judgment was visited on ancient Egypt so that the Hebrews could escape and live, Irenaeus writes: "Unless the Jews had become the slayers of the Lord (which did, indeed, take eternal life away from them), and, by killing the apostles and persecuting the church, had fallen into an abyss of wrath, we could not have been saved" (4.28.3). This is redolent of Paul's argument about Israel's stumbling as the opportunity for the Gentiles' salvation (see Rom. 11:11), but with a judgmental twist that is absent from Paul. The passage goes on: "For as they were saved by the blindness of the Egyptians, so are we, too, by the blindness of the Jews if, indeed, the death of the Lord is the condemnation of those who fastened him to the cross and did not believe his coming, but the salvation of those who believed in him. He responds to his own uncertainty by a generalized reflection on believers and unbelievers in Christ without any reference to Jews or non-Jews.

It is not possible, given the few surviving written testimonies between 50 and 175 C.E., to trace the progress of the idea of Jewish responsibility for the death of Jesus and the persecution of believers in him. There does not seem to be a straight line from the Gospels and Acts to the second-century Apologists, as if the latter simply copied out what they read there and decided to use Pilate as a dating device only, rather than the one who condemned Jesus to death. We do not know the impact of the oral tradition or the lost written tradition except in its results, nor can we know the exacerbation caused by a century and a quarter of unrecorded events. What we can confidently say is that the chief priests and elders of Judea whom John's Gospel charged with Jesus' death have become, in a gentile church, Jews generally. Further, it begins to be said that Jews generally bear the guilt of the crime because their spiritual descendants of the next century have not repudiated it by coming to faith in Christ. By their continued harassments, they have only confirmed it.

An examination of the earliest extant liturgies[7] shows that this theme occurs in them only in the poetic Easter homily of Melito of Sardis (d. ca. 190). This homily was not the fixed formula of any church but probably exerted its influence on Irenaeus and Tertullian. Early baptismal creeds like that which Hippolytus of Rome gives in his *Apostolic Tradition* (ca. 215), later developed into the Apostles' Creed (first so called at a Synod of Milan in 390 and found initially in its present wording in the seventh- or eighth-century Bobbio Missal), confine themselves to the word "suffered" or the phrase "suffered under Pontius Pilate, was crucified, died, and was buried."[8] Melito's sharp departure from the restraint of the creeds and even the Gospels consisted in a succession of fiery images from the Bible establishing that the Jewish *Pesaḥ* (Passover) had been succeeded by the Christian *Pascha*.

Melito writes of "the new and the old, the eternal and temporal, the incorruptible and corruptible, the immortal and the mortal," in a dizzying array of replacement images. And in one passage:

He was put to death. . . . Where was he put to death? In the midst of Jerusalem. Why?

Because he had cured their lame,
because he had cleansed their lepers,

because he had restored sight to the
  blind,
because he had raised their dead.

. . .

O Israel, why have you committed this
unheard-of crime? You have dishonored
him who honored you. . . . you have put to
death him who gave you life! Why did
you do this, O Israel? Was it not for you
that it is written: "You shall not shed innocent blood, lest you die a wretched
death"? . . .

. . .

You were not moved to reverence for
  him
by the withered hand of the paralytic

. . . .

You were not moved to fear . . .
by the dead man he called back from
  the tomb. . . .

No, you took no account of these, but in
order to immolate the Lord as evening
came on, you prepared for him

sharp nails
and false witnesses
and ropes and whips
and vinegar and gall
and sword and pain
as for a bandit who had shed blood.[9]

By Melito's time the tradition is in full cry that will understand all the Hebrew Bible's reproaches to Israel—and they are many—to be directed to Jesus' tormentors, as the chief priests and temple guard were thought to have been. If the Christian-Jewish tension had not continued uninterrupted, the sins laid to Israel's charge by the prophets might not have been put to this use. We do not have in this rhetoric of reproach anything remotely historical. It is part mythical, part angrily existential.

Tertullian and Origen

Tertullian's anti-Judaism often takes the form of describing Jews as "that stiff-necked people, devoid of faith in God."[10] As regards the crucifixion, the North African rhetorician (ca. 200) does not content himself with the charge we have already encountered that the Jews put Jesus to death but says that they "not only rejected him as a stranger but even put him to death as an opponent."[11] This is part of an obscure argument to the effect that the one to come was expected by Jews to be unknown to them. Tertullian makes it part of prophecy that they would destroy him: "It at once follows that he who was unrecognized by them, he whom they put to death, is the one who they were marked down beforehand as going to treat in this fashion."[12] He then quotes at length Isaiah 29:14b joined to 6:9b-10 to prove that Christ went unrecognized because God had promised to render this people blind and deaf. He adds a hint of 1 Corinthians 2:8, where Paul says: "If the rulers of this age knew [the plan of God's wisdom] they would not have crucified the Lord of glory."

Tertullian is far from obscure, however, when he finds Jeremiah's proverbial saying about fathers eating sour grapes and children having their teeth set on edge to apply prophetically to the outcry inserted by Matthew into the Markan narrative: "His blood be upon us and on our children."[13] Tertullian wishes to refute Marcion's statement that "the passion of the cross was never prophesied concerning the Christ of the Creator" and that it was "quite incredible that the Creator should have exposed his Son to that form of death on which he himself had laid a curse."[14] This he does by identifying Isaac's delivering up by his father in a sacrifice as a case of prophecy "by types and figures" and Joseph's persecution by his brothers the same.[15] But he cannot refrain from making Simeon and Levi, the violent slayers of Genesis 49:5-7, stand for the scribes and Pharisees who persecuted Christ, "whom after the murder of the prophets they crucified, and with nails wrought savagely against his sinews."[16] Refuting Marcion's claim that it was "the Christ of the other god who was brought to the cross," Tertullian states that the crucifixion was real and that it was the work of the Jews.[17] He makes the same assumption in commenting on 1 Thessalonians 2:14-16, namely, that they "both killed the Lord and their own prophets."[18]

The denigration of the Jews and Judaism in Tertullian, pervasive and not found only in *Adversus Marcionem*, seems to be a by-product. It derives from his proof that the God of the Hebrew Scriptures could not have been guilty of all that Marcion charged him with. Since it came from somewhere, the Jews of the Bible must have been the offending parties, the source. Contributing to this mythicizing of the Jews were the four Gospels and Luke's volume two, with their outcries by "the crowd" (Mark 15:8-14; Matt. 27:25) or *tois Ioudaiois* (John 19:14; the same as "the chief priests and the guards" of v. 6?) that Jesus should be crucified, in response to which Pilate handed him over (Mark 15:15; Luke 23:25; John 19:16; "to them"). Every detail of Christ's passion was foretold in Scripture, but God was responsible for none of these. The Jews were.[19]

The first hundred years of Christian writing after the New Testament was completed not only make no critical evaluation of the two testaments of Scripture but also make no distinctions among the varied responses of the Hebrews/ Israelites of the Bible to their covenant calling. All the resisters to Moses and the writing prophets and Jesus' learned opponents in the Gospels are lumped together as "the Jews" as if there were no other Jews. The emerging Christians, both outwardly beleaguered and inwardly divided, evidently needed an identifiable opponent to unite them, especially against Marcion's charge that the god of the Bible was an evil god. Their contemporaries the Jews, whom not many of them can have known in an intimate way, served as the occasion. The need for an enemy was the cause.

Origen (d. 253/54), the "first speculative theologian," was born and raised in Alexandria, but we do not know if the knowledge of halakah evidenced in his *On First Principles* was acquired there or on his already extensive travels. We know that Origen had many more contacts with Jews after his move to Caesarea on the seacoast of Palestine. The Samaritans had a colony there in his day. It was the capital of Roman Palestine and had a vigorous pagan culture (to which Origen does not advert). There were certainly Jews, Greek-speaking by and large, who may be presumed to have employed pagan art forms and motifs on their tombs and synagogues, like the Jews elsewhere in the country. Caesarea was resented because the memory of the cruelties of the Bar Kokhba revolt (135 C.E.) was still fresh in the Jewish mind and the opportunities for apostasy and religious syncretism were many.[20]

Origen mentions consulting a Jewish teacher, "the Patriarch Ioullos," whose name Jerome renders as Huillus (Ioudas? Hillel?),[21] but he is not the same as "my Hebrew teacher" to whom Origen frequently refers. This may be a Christian of Jewish origin or a Jew who has no scruple in helping a Christian understand the Scriptures better. For it is abundantly clear that Origen wants to master Jewish hermeneutical techniques for his own Christian purpose. He repeatedly charges Jews with a literal or "carnal" understanding of the Bible while employing Philo's pattern of metaphoric parallel (or typology, commonly called the "allegorical method") without ever adverting to the paradox. Yet he very much wishes to come abreast of the way the Rabbis play word games and utilize common elements and contrasts in biblical narratives. He undoubtedly hopes to best Jewish teachers in argument.[22] At the same time, when his learned pagan opponent Celsus points out absurdities in either testament of Scripture, Origen willingly employs refutations derived from Jewish sources.

The sign of the cross had been a Jewish symbol well before Jesus' crucifixion, appearing in Jewish underground cemeteries in Rome, on Jewish sarcophagi in Jerusalem from the first century B.C.E. to the third century C.E., and in the third-century synagogue at Dura-Europos.[23] Origen says that a Jewish Christian told him that the "sign" of Ezekiel 9:4 was the cruciform Old Hebrew letter *tau*.[24] Like Christian writers before him he compares Isaac to Christ carrying the wood for his own immolation; in this he comes close to a passage in *Genesis Rabbah*.[25] Which

influenced which? Or was there no interrela-
tion? The same may be asked of Moses' upraised
arms (Exod. 17:11) as a symbol of the cross, already used by Pseudo-Barnabas, Justin, and Irenaeus. Origen borrows from Rabbi Eliezer and
Rabbi Akiba the symbolism of Moses' upraised
arms to represent human actions and observance of the law but turns it to mean two peoples: the Christians who elevate what Moses
wrote by understanding it on a high level and
the people who do not see anything deep or
subtle in Moses, thus failing to elevate his arms
or lift them off the ground.[26] The Jews are, once
again, capable of only a literal reading of the
text while Christians perceive the mysteries that
are but hinted at in the Bible. Thus,

> Both the hardened in heart and the igno-
> rant persons belonging to the circumci-
> sion have not believed in our Savior,
> thinking that they are following the lan-
> guage of the prophecies respecting him.
> . . . Seeing none of these things [from
> Zech. 9:10; Isa. 7:15; 11:6, 7] visibly ac-
> complished during the advent of him who
> is believed by us to be the Christ, they did
> not accept our Lord Jesus, but they cruci-
> fied him improperly because he affirmed
> that he was the Christ.[27]

Understanding the Scriptures spiritually, that is,
in allegorical and typological forms, Origen

thinks would have kept them from this unbelief
and its consequences: "For although salvation
and justification came to the Gentiles through
his cross, to the Jews came condemnation and
ruin."[28]

Origen represents Celsus as having discov-
ered a Jew who told Jewish converts to Christianity, "Quite recently, when we punished this
fellow who deluded you, you abandoned the
law of our fathers," and, "as an offender he was
punished by the Jews."[29] Origen answers that it
was no crime for Jesus to abstain from a literal
Sabbath and observances over clean and un-
clean meats, "rather to turn the mind to the
good and true and spiritual law, worthy of
God."[30] In this lengthy treatise the charge sur-
faces that the Jews have suffered and will suffer more than others in the judgment that
hangs over the world "on account of their dis-
belief in Jesus and all their other insults to him.
. . . What nation but the Jews alone has been
banished from its own capital city and the native place of its ancestral worship?"[31] Origen
lays the severity of the punishment of this
"most wicked nation" to their sins committed
against "our Jesus." Celsus must know the
Gospels and some Roman history because he
says that no calamity ever overtook the one
who condemned Jesus. Origen's reply to this is
that "it was not so much Pilate who condemned
him, since he knew that 'out of envy the Jews
had delivered him up,' as the Jewish people.

This nation has been condemned by God and torn in pieces and scattered over the whole earth."[32]

Celsus evidently despises the Jews as a people, saying that they were never of any reputation or account. This Origen hotly denies, pointing out the many centuries during which they enjoyed the divine protection interspersed with their abandonment by God for longer or shorter periods. But God's final and complete desertion of them came in Roman times, when they "committed their greatest sin in killing Jesus. For this, they were entirely abandoned."[33] That theological judgment is tempered with a bit of sober history when, in speaking of the fact that no one sees God with bodily eyes, Origen says that neither those who cried "Crucify him!" nor Pilate, "who received power over Jesus' humanity," could see God the Father directly.[34] The events of the passion were earthly history for Origen, not a fable.

Yet this Alexandrian native at all times also operates theologically in the matter of Jesus' death. His biblical commentaries show him quite capable of critical history, but he never applies these skills to the New Testament accounts of the death of Jesus. These he accepts as sober history without question, taking the reported pressure of Jerusalem Jews (among whom he does not make distinctions) on Pilate to condemn Jesus as equivalent to making them the primary agents of his crucifixion. He derives from this assumption of fact—a fact that horrifies him, given his faith conviction that Jesus is divine as well as human—a providential punishment of later generations of Jews for the sin of their fathers. He was not the first to arrive at this conclusion, but a theory of inherited guilt may have been Origen's chief contribution to the Christian understanding of Jesus' death. This false supposition, in any case, remained firmly in Christian memory.

Eusebius and Fourth-Century Church Fathers

It was some time around 314 that Eusebius, the Greek-speaking bishop of Caesarea in Palestine and admirer of Emperor Constantine, completed *Preparation for the Gospel* in fifteen books.[35] All are extant, but of the *Demonstration of the Gospel* (314–18) only ten of twenty books remain. Eusebius refers to the "Hebrews" from the time of Abraham to Moses, following which they become "Jews"; but then the prophets and Jesus and his disciples become "Hebrews" again. Despite this erratic terminology, Eusebius has the utmost respect for Moses and his laws. He speaks early in his first treatise of "adhering to the God who is honored among the Jews in their customary rites."[36] Before long, however, he refers to the deeds they wrought against Jesus as resulting in the final siege of Jerusalem and their dispersion and bondage in the territory of their enemies.[37] This kind of language is then absent from the rest of the treatise.

For many who know its title but not its content, the *Preparation for the Gospel* is a classic of supersessionism, but it is scarcely that. It is in fact a long preamble to the *Demonstration,* which in turn hopes to answer all reasonable questions from Jewish or Greek inquirers about Christianity. The major line of approach of this second work is that the Mosaic religion was a decline from the primitive cult of the patriarchs, to which Hebrew original the prophets and Jesus returned.

In *Demonstration* Eusebius discovers in "the plot against our Savior Jesus Christ," "that through which and after which all the things above-mentioned [the desolation of Jerusalem predicted by Isaiah in chaps. 1–3] overtook them [i.e., the whole people of the Jews that the prophet accused]."[38] It was the "impiety done to our Savior" that resulted in the sieges of Vespasian and Hadrian, following which Jews "were completely debarred from the place, not even being allowed to tread the soil of Jerusalem."[39] This is supported with a series of totally obscure references to Isaiah. When in book 10, the last one extant, Eusebius marshals the biblical passages he identifies as prophetic of Jesus' passion and death, he names the plotters against him as Judas and "the rulers of the Jews."[40] Applying LXX Psalm 108 (MT 109) to

Matthew's narrative in chap. 26, he understands the text, "Set a wicked man over him, and let Satan stand at his right hand. . . . Let his days be free and let another take his office" (vv. 6, 8), to establish that "a sinful ruler and head was given to the Jewish people, after their presumptuous deeds against the Savior and they were forced to serve strangers and idolators instead of their ancient godly rulers."[41] Having observed Luke's application of this text to the traitor Judas (Acts 1:20), Eusebius proceeds immediately to identify the sinful ruler and head as presumable Rome or its emperor. The presence of "Satan at [the sinner's] right hand," however, is an ominous detail in the use of this psalm in Eucebius's context.

Fourth-century Christian writers evidently had a primary need to assert Christianity's uniqueness against Judaism and paganism. The apologists and theologians thought their faith much closer religiously to that of Israel than that of the empire. They had to find reasons for God's self-revelation in Christ or they would have had the problem of a divine deed that was needless. Christianity's superiority to Judaism was thus a demand of their logic. The need was heightened by the similarities of Christianity to the old religion and the attraction this Jewish cult exercised on their fellow religionists. Establishing Jewish sin and wrongdoing would accomplish two things: absolve deity from the charge of a change of mind and show the

Bible's correctness in its prophetic castigation of Israel's sins. If the Jews had done extreme wrong by working violence on the one whom God had sent them in fulfillment of all prophecy, several things—including accounting for the sufferings of the Jews at Roman hands—would be achieved. That is what made the crucifixion of Jesus by the Jews a kind of theological necessity. His having been done to death by Roman authority, on the contrary, would have been a commonplace of pagan cruelty. There was no place for it in the scheme of prophecy and fulfillment. Providentially speaking, it would not have fit in.

These reflections may help explain without excusing the nodding of three Christian Homers of the fourth and fifth centuries: Ambrose (339–397), John Chrysostom (347–407), and Augustine (363–430). Ambrose had been based in Milan as the *consularis* of Liguria and Aemilia, roughly the position Pilate held, when he was elected as Milan's bishop in 374. Still a catechumen in his thirties, he received in succession baptism and the order of bishop. In resisting the emperor Theodosius's efforts to run a theocratic state, Ambrose opposed the civil rights accorded to Jews, heretics, and pagans that equaled those of Christians, a move of the emperor to show his control over the church. In Julian's brief reign (361–163), churches had been destroyed in Damascus, Beirut, Gaza, and elsewhere without indemnifi-

cation, Ambrose pointed out.[42] He in turn supported a bishop at the head of a mob that had
burned down a synagogue at Callinicum on the
Euphrates. The emperor had commanded that it
be rebuilt. Ambrose's words were: "I claim that
I would have burned that synagogue . . . so
there may be no place in which Christ be denied."[43] For him it was "a place of unbelief." He
asked why Christians should fear Jewish
vengeance, saying: "Whom do they have to
avenge the Synagogue: Christ whom they have
killed, whom they have denied? Or will God the
Father avenge them, whom they do not acknowledge as Father since they do not acknowledge the Son."[44] In a public confrontation in his
cathedral the bishop made the emperor back
down."[45]

There was no understanding of the religious
"other" here, only a charge of the Jews" being
wrong in religion based on a criminal deed centuries before, from which they had no appeal.

They insinuate themselves cleverly among
people . . . disturb the ears of judges and
other public figures, and get on all the better for their impudence. Nor is this a recent
matter with them but a longstanding evil
going back to their origins. In time past
they even persecuted the Lord and Savior
within the praetorium, condemning him
before the judgment of the one who
presided (Matt. 27:2ff.). In that place inno-

cence was oppressed by the Jews, religion condemned, what was hidden betrayed. For with the killing of Christ all the truth and justice was condemned; he is innocence itself and thus the religion of holiness, too, and mystery.[46]

Almost contemporaneous with Ambrose was the Greek-speaking Antiochian John Chrysostom. His rhetorical excesses in the eight sermons he preached against the Jews immediately after his ordination as a presbyter of Antioch (aged thirty-seven) are well known. Fearful of the influence of the Arians upon Catholics, he launched a series against them but shortly interrupted it in the fall of 386 with two sermons against the Jews as their holy days came on. He identified as "a disease flourishing within the body of the church" the attendance of "many who belong to us and say they believe in our teaching, attend their festivals, and even share in their celebrations and join in their fasts."[47] He was convinced that such participation amounted to apostasy, although an explanatory detail may be the evidence that there was a late survival of early judaizing tendencies in Christian Antioch.[48]

Chrysostom was brutally harsh in his descriptions of the Jews as ungrateful to God, given to drunkenness and overeating, licentiousness, and dancing with naked feet in the marketplace. He could not let stand the opinion of many that the Jews are holy and that oaths taken in synagogues are especially sacred; that opinion must be uprooted. As part of his polemic he spoke of one who worships Christ dragging a person off "to the haunts of the Jews who crucified [Jesus]."[49] "Not only the synagogue but also the souls of Jews are the dwelling places of demons."[50] "Do anything to rescue [your brother] from the devil's snare and deliver him from the fellowship of the Christ-killers."[51] Chrysostom identified those Jews who are now fasting with the people who shouted "Crucify him! Crucify him!" (Luke 23:21) and "His blood be on us and on our children" (Matt. 27:23, 25). "Is it not folly for those who worship the crucified to celebrate festivals with those who crucified him?"[52] "They killed the son of your Lord, and yet you dare to gather with them in the same place? When the one who was killed by them honors you by making you a brother and fellow heir, you dishonor him by revering his murdered, those who crucified him, and by attending their festival assemblies."[53]

John Chrysostom was not always as violent as this in his condemnation of the Jews. His best argument in favor of Christianity is already foreshadowed in Homily 7. The eclipse of the Jewish law's validity is "*not* because of the sins of the Jews but because of its own inherent imperfection which required the new dispensation of Christ."[54] A new order of sacrifice was instituted, Chrysostom gets around to saying, as a transformation of the old: the order of Abraham's contemporary Melchizedek, which Hebrews 5:6 identifies as the order of Christ.[55] This explanation cannot be expected to have given much comfort to the Jews of Antioch who were hearing of the slanders against them from the dual-attendance Christians against whom the fiery new preacher's remarks were directed. But it is the latter that live in Jewish memory. Christians, meanwhile, tend not to have heard of Chrysostom's anti-Judaism, though the poisonous remarks he authored became part of their anonymous heritage.

The immensely influential Augustine entertained no thought that the Jews could lose the stigma of having disbelieved in Jesus. "You have killed Christ in your ancestors," he wrote. Clearly he thought of it as a collective guilt.[56] It is certainly easy for us to put down the Jews' lack of faith to the root cause of free choice, he wrote, "for many . . . willed to believe neither him nor those he raised from the dead."[57] Despite the severity of his judgment, Augustine was convinced it was the right one. His theory of grace forced him to believe that the Jewish people over four centuries had had the possibility of believing held out to them by a God who forces no one's will, and they had freely rejected the option. What we would call "social factors," or the possibility of God's grace given them to persevere in covenanted peoplehood, do not figure in Augustine's reckoning. In the world of his day, no religion showed itself capable of making such allowances. The wrong were simply wrongheaded.

What Augustine could and did say, in a sermon delivered in the last five years of his long life, was that "what the Jews read [in Scripture] they do not understand." By "understanding" he meant interpreting the Bible spiritually as Christians did. He was not so foolish as to think Jews could be invited just to read their sacred writings and thereby come to faith. On his own principle he required that they first believe so as to understand.[58] What we must do, Augustine says, is preach to them in love, whether they hear us willingly or not, "not with the presumption of insult (*insultando*) but with an awesome rejoicing (*exsultando*)." But the preaching in love he counseled was never purged of insult, largely because Christians were incapable of recognizing the wounds they caused by the grounds for argument they chose.

Pope Gregory the Great

Aside from Ambrose's literally fiery opinion on the Callinicum synagogue expressed to Theodosius, little in the writings of the church fathers tells of their relations with actual Jews. Gregory, bishop of Rome (590–604), provides an exception. It is a welcome one, because in the thirty or so of his eight hundred letters that deal with the Jews he shows himself solicitous

for justice in their regard and the preservation
of their rights under Roman law.[59] He favors
their becoming Christian, as one might expect,
but is set against anything smacking of duress,
knowing that such "conversions" cannot be expected to be meaningful. From Gregory's correspondence much can be learned about Jewish
life toward the end of the sixth century: the
deep involvement of Jews in the slave trade,
their living in amity with Christians in some
regions and being dealt with sharply, even
cruelly, by them in others, and the Jewish-
Christian tensions that arose from close living,
like churches and synagogues troubling each
other by the volume of their sons.

When Pope Gregory acts as a theologian
rather than an administrator, his voluminous
writings betray no sympathy whatever for Jews
or a wish to receive them into the church. In
referring to them he uses such terms as superstition, vomit, perdition, and *perfidia*, and
describes them as the enemies of Christ.[60]
[Gregory's] practical treatment of problems
connected with the presence of Jews in Christian society," the Tel Aviv historian Shlomo
Simonsohn says correctly, "laid the foundations
of papal Jewry policy in the Middle Ages."[61] In
his allegorical reading of the Bible wild asses,
unicorns, basilisks, and serpents turn out to
stand for Jews. This wise and practical renderer
of judgments that protect Jews is the captive of
a theological position which, carried to its

logical extremes, resulted in harassment of them and even bodily harm. The bishop of Rome does not see that. There is right in religion and there is wrong. The Jews, regrettably, are wrong; and an inerrant Scripture, every verse of which contains a secret meaning, is employed to lay this bare.

Conclusion

What can be said to summarize the attribution of responsibility for Jesus' death to the Jews by the church fathers of the years 100–600? First, they thought it clearly taught in the New Testament. For this they relied on the Acts of the Apostles as much as on the Gospels. That Pilate sentenced Jesus—whatever the measure of temple priestly encouragement—was thought to be a nonfact except in the creedal statement that served to date Jesus' sufferings.

It came to be assumed very early in the patristic age that every member of subsequent generations of Jews concurred in this wicked deed. There was, of course, no evidence for this assumption, but it was thought that their failure to become Christians proved it. The latter argument was based on empirical observation, coupled with some harassment at the hands of Jews, even though the conclusion drawn was false. The main argument was a deduction from biblical data. The prophets had foretold Jesus' sufferings at the hands of his own people, it was supposed, because of all the texts that spoke of the abuse heaped on an innocent one by fellow Jews. It had all come to pass in the case of the singularly just Jesus. His rejection at the hands of others was freely willed by them in the fulfillment of prophecy. The failure of later generations of Jews to believe in the cross and resurrection as saving events confirmed the hardness of heart of their first-century forebears.

The whole construct was a totally false elaboration of a partially valid myth. But this fact gave the Jewish people of the patristic era, particularly from Constantine's day onward, no consolation whatever. They began a centuries-long history of being stigmatized as the killers of Christ on the cross, when in fact they would have repudiated to a person the small number of Jews in power who had had a part in the deed.

Abbreviations

ANF	Ante-Nicene Fathers
b.	Babylonian Talmud tractates
CChr	Corpus Christianorum
CSEL	Corpus scriptorum ecclesiasticorum latinorum
DS	Denzinger-Schönmetzer, Enchiridion symbolorum
ET	English translation
GCS	Grieschischen christlichen Schriftsteller
HTR	*Harvard Theological Review*
IEJ	*Israel Exploration Journal*
JBL	*Journal of Biblical Literature*
LXX	Septuagint
m.	Misnah tractates
MT	Masoretic text
PG	J. Migne, Patrum graecorum
PL	J. Migne, Patrum latinorum
Sanh.	*Sanhedrin*
SC	Sources chrétiennes
y.	Jerusalem Talmud tractates

Citations without a series or alternative publication data given are from the Loeb Classical Library.

Notes

Introduction

1. Gerald G. O'Collins makes the point successfully when he argues that, although the "resurrection is a real bodily event involving the person of Jesus of Nazareth," the resurrection of Jesus "is not an event *in* space and time and hence should not be called historical" since "we should require an historical event to be something significant that is known to have happened in our space-time continuum." See his "Is the Resurrection an 'Historical Event'?" *Heythrop Journal* 8 (1967) 381–87; the quotations are from pp. 381, 384.

1. The Crucifixion of Jesus: How, Why, and by Whom?

1. See Mark 15:15-19. Matthew at 27:28-29 edits Mark by making it a scarlet military cloak and first placing the reed in Jesus' right hand, scepterlike; Luke uniquely, at 23:7-11, has Pilate send Jesus to Herod (Antipas), there to receive this contemptuous treatment from him and his soldiers while the chief priests and scribes stand by accusingly.

2. See John 19:1-5b. For a careful exploration of these and other details, see Raymond E. Brown, *The Death of the Messiah: From Gethsemane to the Grave: A Commentary on the Passion Narratives of the Four Gospels*, 2 vols. (New York: Doubleday, 1994).

3. Mark 10:33-34. The other predictions of his death, less detailed, are in 8:31 and 9:31. Matthew retains them at 16:21; 17:22-23; 20:18-19; Luke at 9:22, 24; 18:31-33. John has no such prophecies by Jesus.

4. For exhaustive detail on how and by whom crucifixion was administered in the ancient world see Martin Hengel, *Crucifixion,* trans. John Bowden (Philadelphia: Fortress Press, 1977).

5. Herodotus 9.120 (ET, A. D. Godley, 1924; 4.298). See also 1.128, where Astyages the Median impaled (*aneskolopise*) the Magians (*magoi*), interpreters of dreams, who had persuaded him to let Cyrus go free.

6. Seneca, *To Marcia on Consolation* 20.3 (ET, John W. Basore, 1935); 2.68.

7. Josephus, *Jewish War* 5.451 (ET, H. St. J. Thackeray, 1928; 3.340).

8. Ibid., 7.202-3 (3.563).

9. Pseudo-Manetho, *Apotelesmatica* 4.198ff., as cited by Hengel, *Crucifixion,* 9, n. 20 (translation adapted).

10. Sources are given in Hengel, *Crucifixion,* 9-10, nn. 21-23. A brief chapter there (pp. 11-14) describes Prometheus's mythic crucifixion as it is dealt with by the satirist Lucian in his mockery of the gods, *Prometheus* (ET, A. M. Harmon, 1915; 2.242-45), and the account in the *History* of Diodorus of Sicily (d. after 36 B.C.E.) of the crucifixion of Lycurgus by the god Dionysius (3.65.5-6; ET, C. H. Oldfather, 1935;

2.298–301). The cruel punishment that had grown familiar to the Greeks from the Persian and Macedonian wars was retrojected onto the myths that in earlier days did not speak of it. Lucian, incidentally, makes a jab against the Christians in his *Passing of Peregrinus* 13, 11 (ET, 5.14–15, 12–13): "They worship that crucified sophist and live according to his laws. . . . The man who was crucified in Palestine because he introduced this new cult into the world."

11. Titus Livius, *History* 22.13.9 (ET, B. O. Foster, 1929; 5.244); cf. 28.37.3 At times the flogging preceded execution by some other means. Antigonus, the last Jewish king in the Hasmonean line (d. 38 B.C.E.), was beheaded after humiliating flagellation, "the only king to endure this at Roman hands." Dio Cassius 49.22.6 (ET, Earnest Cary, 1917; 386, 388).

12. See Suetonius, "Nero" 49.2 (ET, 2.178); Dio Cassius 2.6; 1.68.

13. See J. W. Hewitt, "The Use of Nails in Crucifixion," *HTR* 25 (1932) 29–45; cf. Philo *On Dreams* 2.213 (ET, F. H. Colson and G. H. Whitaker, 5.538); Plutarch *Morals* 499D (ET, W. C. Helmbold, 6.730); Lucan *The Civil War* 6.543–49 (ET, J. D. Duff, 344–34); Seneca "On the Happy Life" 19.3 (ET, John W. Basore, 2.48). Several of these speak of "nailing up" on victim and Lucan of the "nails that pierced the hands [*Insertum manibus*]." A crucified man was found in Jerusalem with a nail still in his heel-bone. See N. Haas, "Anthropological Observations on the Skeletal Remains from Giv'at ha-Mivtar," *IEJ* 20 (1970) 38–59. On the use of nails see also Josef Blinzler, *The Trial of Jesus,* trans. I. And F. McHugh (ET of 2d ed.; Westminster, Md.: Newman, 1959), 250, 264–65.

14. Seneca, *Epistle* 101, "On the Futility of Planning Ahead," 12 (ET, Richard H. Gummere, 1925; 3.164–65); H. Fulda, *Das Kreuz und die Kreuzigung: Eine antiquarische Untersuchung* (Breslau, 1878), a work not available to me.

15. Minucius Felix, *Octavius*, ed. C. Halm; CSEL 2 (Vienna, 1867), 3–56 (ET, *The Octavius of Marcus Minucius Felix,* G. W. Clarke; New York and Paramus, N.J.: 1974).

16. See *Octavius* 8–12 for a lurid catalog of supposed Christian practices, which at 13.5 are described as "doting [*anilis*] superstition."

17. Ibid., 9.4; the phrase is *cruces ligna feralia*. See 29.2 for the charge that Christians worship a criminal (*hominem noxium*) and his cross.

18. Ibid., 29.7; quotation from 23.11 (Clarke, 24.6).

19. M. Tullius Cicero, *Against Verres* 2.5.64 (ET, L. H. G. Greenwood, 1935; 2.650–51). Paragraphs 65 and 66 contain a description of the way one crucifixion was carried out.

20. Some interpret the phrase "hung on a tree" to mean impaled on a stake. The Israelite punishment of dropping a heavy stone on the victim or something like it is obviously understood to be the proper means of execution (see *m. Sanh.* 6:4), although how widely it was practiced is not known. The treatment of corpses recommended in Deuteronomy was a warning to others, as in Josh. 8:9; 10:26. The Philistines nailed Saul's headless body to the wall of Beth-shan (1 Sam. 31:10), which may have been equivalent to what the Jews proscribed as "hanging on the wood" (Deut. 21:22-23).

21. Gal. 3:13-14.

22. See Heb. 12:2.

23. *War* 1.97, 113; cf. *Antiquities* 13.380, 410–11.

24. Y. Yadin, *"Pesher Nahum* (4QpNahum) Reconsidered," *IEJ* 21 (1971) 1–12; against his view see J. M. Baumgarten, "Does *tlh* in the Temple Scroll Refer to Crucifixion?" *JBL* 91 (1972) 472–81.

25. See the *baraita* in *b. Sanh.* 46b.

26. In *m. Sanh.* 6.4; see *y. Sanh.* 23c.

27. *m. Sanh.* 6.4.

28. Ibid.

29. Y. Yadin, "Epigraphy and Crucifixion," *IEJ* 23 (1973) 18–22. N. Haas, a medical doctor in Israel, has a different theory, namely, that the feet were nailed onto a cleat of olive wood as the victim hung upright (*IEJ* 20 [1970]: 38–59). He assumed in this article the use of the *sediculum* or saddle between the buttocks.

30. For a listing of those who favor and disfavor the opinion that this passage contains interpolated features, see my *Jesus on Trial: The Development of the Passion Narratives and Their Historical and Ecumenical Implications* (Philadelphia: Fortress Press, 1973), 4–5, n. 4. An article sustaining authenticity is Otto Michel's "Fragen zu 1 Thessaloniker 2:14-16: Anti-jüdische Polemik bei Paulus," in *Antijudaismus im Neuen Testament? Exegetische und systematische Beiträge,* ed. W. P. Eckert, et al. (Munich: Kaiser, 1967). Opposing it is Birger A. Pearson, "1 Thessalonians 2:13-16: A Deutero-Pauline Interpretation," *HTR* 64 (1971) 79–94, who cites Baur, Holtzmann, and A. Ritschl as of the same opinion.

31. See Mark 12:17; Matt. 22:21; Luke 20:25.

32. Luke has two, adding to that before the high priest and a Council one with the Galilean tetrarch, Herod Antipas (Luke 23:6-12).

33. Cf. Mark 15:26; Matt. 27:37; Luke 23:38. The wording varies slightly in each case.

34. For the evidence on the Pharisees' thoroughgoing political as well as religious concern, see Anthony J. Saldarini, *Pharisees, Scribes and Sadducees in Palestinian Society: A Sociological Approach* (Wilmington, Del.: Michael Glazier, 1988), 79–106.

35. E. P. Sanders has collected evidence that would indicate that Jesus' statements and symbolic gesture of destruction were related to an end-time hope of the period for a "new Jerusalem." See *Jesus and Judaism* (Philadelphia: Fortress Press, 1985), 77–91.

36. For a good discussion of this term and its compass, see E. P. Sanders, *Jewish Law from Jesus to the Mishnah: Five Studies* (Philadelphia: Trinity Press International, 1990), 57–67.

37. See Richard Horsley, *Jesus and the Spiral of Violence* (Minneapolis: Fortress Press, 1993).

2. How Jesus' Death Came to Be Seen as Redemptive

1. See E. P. Sanders, *Jesus and Judaism* (Philadelphia: Fortress Press, 1985), 103.

2. For a theory on the early recognition of Jesus as the Christ, see Terrance Callan, *The Origins of Christian Faith* (New York: Paulist Press, 1994), esp. pp. 7–35.

3. "For all" would seem to be the proper translation of *anti pollōn* here, in a parallel with *hyper pantōn* in 1 Tim. 2:5-6 and Rom. 8:32. See a note on the translation of *pro multis* as "for all" in the Roman Rite in *Third Progress Report on the Revision of the Roman Missal*

(Washington, D.C.: International Commission on English in the Liturgy, 1992), 152–54.

4. Sam K. Williams, *Jesus' Death as Saving Event : The Background and Origin of a Concept*, Harvard Dissertations in Religion 2 (Missoula, Mont.: Scholars, 1975), 81, 89. This work analyzes the postbiblical writings to see if the cult of the Maccabean martyrs underlay the concept of Jesus' atoning death. It concludes that the pre-Pauline fragment represented by Rom. 3:25-26 derives from the *hilastērion* (means of expiation) concept in the apocryphal 4 Maccabees.

5. Ibid., 248–53, where Williams tries his best.

6. See the helpful article of Daniel Schwartz of the Hebrew University, Jerusalem, "Two Pauline Allusions to the Redemptive Mechanism of the Crucifixion," *JBL* 102 (1983) 259–68.

7. Eugene Weiner and Anita Weiner, *The Martyr's Conviction*, Brown Judaic Studies 203 (Atlanta: Scholars, 1990), 47.

8. Charles B. Cousar, *A Theology of the Cross: The Death of Jesus in the Pauline Letters*, Overtures to Biblical Theology (Minneapolis: Fortress Press, 1990), 25. See also p. 26.

9. For a discussion of this passage, with ample bibliography, see ibid., 40–41.

10. Kenneth Grayston, *Dying We Live: A New Enquiry into the Death of Christ in the New Testament* [New York: Oxford Univ. Press, 1990), 47. This work is basically an exegetical exploration of all the texts touching on Christ's death or dying and its effects as interpreted in faith by early believers in him.

3. How Jesus' Death Was Blamed on "the Jews"

1. *2 Apology* 12; cf. *1 Apology* 1.1. See G. Rauschen, *S. Justini apologiae duae* (Bonn, 1904) (ET, Thomas B. Falls, New York: Fathers of the Church, 1948; 12, 33).

2. Early in the reign of Marcus Aurelius, according to Eusebius's *Church History* 4.16.7 (SC 31, 44, 55, 73; G. Bardy et al., Paris, 1952–87; 31.192). See "The Martyrdom of the Holy Martyrs, Justin, Chariton [and Others]," trans. M. Dods, in A. Roberts and J. Donaldson, eds., ANF 1 (New York, 1908), 305–6.

3. See "Acts of Pilate" in Frederic Huidekoper, *Indirect Testimony of History to the Genuineness of the Gospels* (New York: David G. Francis, 1887), 105–42; also, "The Report of Pilate [to Tiberius]," 142–49.

4. See *b. Sanh.* 43a; for a discussion of the few possible talmudic references to Jesus of Nazareth, see John P. Meier, *A Marginal Jew: Rethinking the Historical Jesus,* vol. 1 (New York: Doubleday, 1991), 106–7, 246–47, who also discusses the story of Jesus' illegitimacy reported by Origen in Celsus's *True Discourse* (ca. 178) and the slanderous ninth-century (?) *Sepher Toledoth Yeshu.*

5. Commonly referred to as *Against Heresies (Adversus Haereses)* but entitled by Irenaeus *The Refutation and the Overthrow of the Knowledge Falsely So Called,* PG 7 (ET, ANF 1.315–567). An incomplete critical edition of the Latin translation augmented by Greek and Armenian fragments is Adelin Rousseau and Louis Doutreleau, SC 264, 293, 294 (Paris, 1979–). Critical apparatus is given in vol. 100, 152, 153, 210, 211, 263. Irenaeus's books 3 and 4 meet the Marcionite challenge head on.

6. *Adversus Haereses* 3.12.6.

7. The early third-century church-order treatise *Catholic Teaching of the Twelve Apostles and Holy Disciples of Our Savior* (*Didascalia*) is the work in Greek of a bishop of northern Syria. It contains a doxology after chap. 26 praising "Jesus Christ of Nazareth . . . who was crucified in the days of Pontius Pilate, and slept [died]" (R. H. Connolly, *Didascalia Apostolorum* [Oxford: Clarendon, 1929], 258–59).

8. See J. N. D. Kelly, *Early Christian Creeds,* 3d ed. (New York: McKay, 1972), 149–50, where it is identified as a means of rooting the event of Jesus' death in history. The texts are given in Greek and Latin in DS §§10–64.

9. *Peri Pascha,* found without title on a Chester Beatty Papyrus shared between Dublin and Ann Arbor and published by Campbell Bonner (Studies and Documents; Philadelphia: University of Pennsylvania Press, 1940). See the critical edition of S. G. Hall (Oxford Early English Texts, 1979) and the rhythmic (but partial) translation of Matthew J. O'Connell in Lucien Deiss, *Springtime of the Liturgy* (Collegeville, Minn.: Liturgical, 1979), 106–7, cited here. Eric Werner writes of "Melito of Sardes, the First Poet of Deicide," *Hebrew Union College Annual* 37 (1966) 191–210. In chap. 21, in a chronology of Jesus' last six days not supported by the Gospels, Pilate is exculpated, and it is further written: "Herod commanded that he could be crucified" (p. 191).

10. Tertullian, *Adversus Marcionem,* ed. and trans. Ernest Evans, 2 vols. (Oxford: Clarendon, 1972), 2.18.1; cf. 15.1. Tertullian's anti-Judaism has been explored in detail by David Efroymson, "Tertullian's Anti-Judaism

and Its Role in His Theology" (Ph.D. diss., Temple University, 1976).

11. Tertullian, *Adversus Marcionem* 3.6.2.

12. Ibid., 6.4.

13. Matt. 27:25. Referring to Jer. 31:29 (again in Ezek. 18:2), Tertullian acknowledges at length that the prophets use this proverb to make the *opposite* point, namely, that inherited guilt is henceforth to yield to personal responsibility, but he makes the legal cavil, "yet without prejudice to that decree which was afterwards to be made." Matthew is recording the fathers' willingness to "call down this judgment upon themselves, *His blood be on our heads and on our children's* [Matt. 27:25]," Tertullian maintains, "if you were to accept the Gospel in its true form [i.e., as a record of truth]" (2.15.2–3). The same text is cited, along with John 19:12 ("If you release him you are no friend of Caesar") in Tertullian's *Adversus Iudaeos* 8.18, CChr, Series Latina 2, *Tertulliani Opera,* Part II, ed. A. Gerlo (Turnhout: Brepols, 1954), 1364.

14. *Adversus Marcionem* 3.18.1.

15. Ibid., 2–3; cf. *Adversus Iudaeos* 10.6.

16. *Adversus Iudaeos* 3.18.5.

17. Ibid., 3.23.5–6, 1.

18. Ibid., 5.15.1–2.

19. See *An Answer to the Jews* 13, for which the translator, S. Thelwall, provides the heading "Argument from the Destruction of Jerusalem and Desolation of Judea," in ANF, 3.168. Most authors think that chaps. 9–14, which conclude the treatise, were added by another hand, taken from *Adversus Marcionem* 3.

20. See N. R. M. de Lange, *Origen and the Jews: Studies in Jewish-Christian Relations in Third-Century*

Palestine (Cambridge: Cambridge Univ. Press, 1976), 7–12.

21. Origen, prologue to *Commentary on the Psalms* (*PG* 12.1056).

22. See *Epistle to Africanus* 5 (*PG* 11.–61); cf. *Against Celsus* 1.45, 49, 55; 6.29 (*PG* 12.744, 752–63, 13.37; ET, Henry Chadwick, *Origen: Contra Celsum* [Cambridge: Cambridge Univ. Press, 1975]). For his familiarity with the Judaism of his time, see the collected texts in Gustave Bardy, "Les traditions juives dans l'oeuvre d'Origène," *Revue biblique* (1925) 217–52.

23. See Erich Dinkler, *Signum Crucis* (Tübingen: Moh/Siebeck, 1967), 1–54.

24. *Selecta on Ezekiel* (*PG* 13.801A), cited by de Lange, *Origen,* 116.

25. *Homily on Genesis* 8.6 (*PG* 12.206; GCS 6.81.6). See *Genesis Rabbah* 66.3.

26. *Homily on Exodus* 11.4 (*PG* 12.578); *On John* 28.5.

27. *On First Principles* 4.2.1 (H. Crouzel and M. Simonetti, SC 268 [Paris, 1980] 293–94, 296; ET, G. W. Butterworth, London: SPCK, 1936; 269, 270).

28. *Homily on Leviticus* 3.1 (*PG* 12.423).

29. *Against Celsus* 2.4, 5.

30. Ibid., 7.

31. Ibid., 8; the same relation is established between Jesus' death and the destruction of Jerusalem in 4.22, the latter event being placed forty-two years after the crucifixion. A novel explanation is given of Jesus' prayer in the garden that the cup of suffering pass from him (Luke 22:42): that the Jews might be delivered from the calamities their sins against him would bring on (see *Against Celsus* 2.25).

32. *Against Celsus* 34.

33. Ibid., 4.32. In 7.8 he describes them as "without a prophet since the advent of Jesus. For the Holy Spirit, as people are well aware, has forsaken them because they acted impiously against God and against the one prophesied by the prophets among them."

34. Ibid., 7.43.

35. Eusebius, *Preparation for the Gospel,* ed. E. des Places, SC 206, 228, 262, 266, 215, 369, 292, 307, 338 (Paris, 1948–87; ET, Edwin Hamilton Gifford; 2 vols.; Oxford: Clarendon, 1903).

36. *Preparation* 1.2.5c (ET, 1.6).

37. Ibid., 3a (ET, 1.10).

38. Eusebius, *Proof* 2.3.37 (ET, 77–79).

39. Ibid., 84.

40. Ibid., 10.1 (ET, 196) and 10.2 (ET, 201).

41. Ibid., 10.3 (ET, 205).

42. *Epistle* 40.15 (*PL* 16.1107).

43. Ibid., 8 (*PL* 16.1104).

44. Ibid., 26 (*PL* 16.1110).

45. Theodosius's protection of the Jews and their meetings is defended at law against "the excesses of those who under the name of the Christian religion are committing illegal actions, or attempting to destroy or ruin synagogues" (*Codex Theodosianus,* ed. T. Mommsen and P. Meyer [Berlin: Weidmann, 1905], 16.8.9).

46. Ambrose, *Sermon 7* (*PL* 17.618).

47. John (Chrysostom) of Antioch, *Against the Jews,* Homily 1.1 (*PG* 48.844). Robert Wilken has translated homilies 1 and 8 in Wayne A. Meeks and Robert L. Wilken, *Jews and Christians in Antioch in the First Four Centuries of the Common Era,* SBL Sources for Biblical Study 13 (Missoula, Mont.: Scholars, 1978), 86.

48. See Marcel Simon, *Verus Israel: A Study of the Relations of Christians and Jews in the Roman Empire, 135–425* (New York: Oxford Univ. Press, 1968), 379–80.

49. *Against the Jews,* Homily 1.3 (*PG* 48.847. ET, Wilken, *Jews and Christians,* 91).

50. Ibid., 4 (*PG* 48.849; ET, 92). Cf. 6 (*PG* 48.862; ET, 98).

51. Ibid., 4 (*PG* 48.849; ET, 93).

52. Ibid., 5 (*PG* 48.850; ET, 94).

53. Ibid., 7 (*PG* 48.854; ET, 100).

54. Gerhart Ladner, "Aspects of Patristic Anti-Judaism," *Viator: Medieval and Renaissance Studies* 2 (1971) 360.

55. *Oratio* (Homily) 12.45 (*PG* 48.921ff.). Hebrews at that place is citing Ps. 110 (LXX 109): 4.

56. *A Sermon against the Jews* 8.11 (*PL* 42.60).

57. *On the Gift of Perseverance* 9.23 (*PL* 45.1005–6). I owe this citation and the preceding one to Ladner (who does not give an English version), with an assist from Robert Wilken.

58. Enunciated clearly in his *Sermon* 43.3, 4 (*PL* 38.255): "A person says to me, 'Let me understand that I may believe,' to which I reply: 'Believe, that you may understand.'"

59. James Parkes devotes several pages to a breakdown of fully half of Gregory's letters in *The Conflict of the Church and the Synagogue: A Study in the Origins of Antisemitism* (London: Soncino, 1934), 210–21. See now Shlomo Simonsohn, *The Apostolic See and the Jews: Documents: 492–1404,* Studies and Texts 94 (Toronto: Pontifical Institute of Medieval Studies, 1988). This eight-volume work gives documents from the Vatican Archives dating from Gelasius I (d. 496) to Julius III (d. 1555).

60. Simonsohn, *Apostolic See*, Documents 5, 12, 13, 23, 24, 25, 26.

61. Idem, *The Apostolic See and the Jews: History*, Studies and Texts 109 (Toronto: Pontifical Institute of Medieval Studies, 1991), 10.

For Further Reading

Boys, Mary C. *Has God Only One Blessing? Judaism as a Source of Christian Self-Understanding.* New York: Paulist, 2000.

Cousar, Charles B. *A Theology of the Cross: The Death of Jesus in the Pauline Letters.* Overtures to Biblical Theology. Minneapolis: Fortress Press, 1990.

Crossan, John Dominic. *Who Killed Jesus? Exposing the Roots of Anti-Semitism in the Gospel Story of the Death of Jesus.* San Francisco: HarperSanFrancisco, 1995.

————, and Jonathan L. Reed. *Excavating Jesus: Beneath the Stones, Behind the Texts.* San Francisco: HarperSanFrancisco, 2001.

Hall, Douglas John. *The Cross in Our Context: Jesus and the Suffering World.* Minneapolis: Fortress Press, 2003.

Hanson, K. C., and Douglas E. Oakman. *Palestine in the Time of Jesus: Social Structures and Social Conflicts with CD-ROM.* Minneapolis: Fortress Press, 2002.

Hengel, Martin. *Crucifixion.* Translated by John Bowden. Philadelphia: Fortress Press, 1977.

Horsley, Richard A., and Neal Asher Silberman. *The Message and the Kingdom: How Jesus and Paul Ignited a Revolution and Transformed the Ancient World.* Minneapolis: Fortress Press, 2002.

Malina, Bruce J., and Richard L. Rohrbaugh. *Social-Science Commentary on the Synoptic Gospels.* 2d ed. Minneapolis: Fortress Press, 2003.

Meier, John P. *A Marginal Jew: Rethinking the Historical Jesus.* Anchor Bible Reference Library. New York: Doubleday, 1991.

Neyrey, Jerome H. *The Passion according to Luke: A Redaction Study of Luke's Soteriology.* New York: Paulist, 1985.

Patterson, Stephen J. *Beyond the Passion: Rethinking the Death and Life of Jesus.* Minneapolis: Fortress Press, 2004.

Rivkin, Ellis. *What Crucified Jesus?* Nashville: Abingdon, 1984.

Sanders, E. P. *Jesus and Judaism.* Philadelphia: Fortress Press, 1985.

Stegemann, Wolfgang, Bruce J. Malina, and Gerd Theissen, editors. *The Social Setting of Jesus and the Gospels.* Minneapolis: Fortress Press, 2002.

Theissen, Gerd. *The Shadow of the Galilean: The Quest of the Historical Jesus in Narrative Form.* Translated by John Bowden. Philadelphia: Fortress Press, 1987.

————, and Annette Merz. *The Historical Jesus: A Comprehensive Guide.* Translated by John Bowden. Minneapolis: Fortress Press, 1998.

Vermes, Geza. *Jesus in His Jewish Context.* Minneapolis: Fortress Press, 2003.

————. *Jesus the Jew: A Historian's Reading of the Gospels.* Philadelphia: Fortress Press, 1981.

Wright, N. T. *The Contemporary Quest for Jesus.* Facets. Minneapolis: Fortress Press, 2003.

————. *The Resurrection of the Son of God.* Christian Origins and the Question of God 3. Minneapolis: Fortress Press, 2003.

Zannoni, Arthur C., editor. *Jews and Christians Speak of Jesus.* Minneapolis: Fortress Press, 1994.

Questions for Study

Introduction

1. If thousands upon thousands were crucified in the ancient Mediterranean world, why did Christians come to assign a special significance to Jesus' death?

Chapter 1

1. Which groups of people were the primary victims of Roman crucifixion?

2. What did you learn about crucifixion as a form of torture and execution that you didn't know before?

3. In what ways do the New Testament writings connect Jesus' death and resurrection?

4. How do the Gospel accounts of Jesus' Passion (arrest, trial, beatings, and crucifixion)

differ from the references to Jesus' death in Paul's letters?

5. How does Sloyan characterize the nature of the Gospel accounts of the Passion? Do you agree or disagree? Why? How would you formulate it differently?

6. What motivated Pilate to order Jesus' execution?

7. How may Jesus' "action in the temple" (see Mark 11:15-19) have been a factor in his arrest?

8. Why would many peasants in Judea and Galilee have been suspicious of the high priestly families in Jerusalem and their power?

Chapter 2

1. How did Jesus' death come to be seen as happening "for our sins"?

2. How are Judean martyrs portrayed in the books of Maccabees, especially in 1 and 2 Maccabees?

3. What differences do you find in the Gospels with regard to responsibility for Jesus' death?

4. How might Jesus' proclamation of the kingdom of God have been one of the factors that led to his death?

5. If the prevailing messianic expectation in the first century was that of a Davidic military leader, why did the earliest Christians come to call Jesus the Messiah (Christ)?

6. According to Sloyan, what role did the sacrificial system of the Jerusalem temple have in the early Christian interpretation of Jesus' death?

Chapter 3

1. Who were the first Christian writers (post-New Testament) to take for granted that "the Jews" were responsible for Jesus' death? When did they write?

2. What teachings of John Chrysostom often cause him to be identified as among the anti-Jewish church fathers?

3. In what ways does Jesus' death speak to victims of state-sponsored torture and execution, the suppression of dissent, and challenges to abusive authority?